Real Cooking for Kids

Inside-Out Spaghetti, Lucky Duck, and More Recipes for the Junior Chef

By Rob Seideman

RUNNING PRESS

PHILADELPHIA · LONDON

Dedicated to the thousands of children who have attended Cooking School of Aspen.
It's to your endless enthusiasm and limitless capabilities that we owe the inspiration for this book.

9   8   7   6   5   4   3   2   1
Digit on the right indicates the number of this printing

Library of Congress Cataloging-in-Publication Number 2002100478

ISBN 0-7624-1323-9

Cover and interior design and illustrations by Corinda Cook
Edited by Melissa Wagner
Typography: Imago

This book may be ordered by mail from the publisher. Please include $2.50 for postage and handling.
But try your bookstore first!

Running Press Book Publishers
125 South Twenty-second Street
Philadelphia, Pennsylvania 19103-4399

Visit us on the web!
www.runningpress.com

Table of Contents ▲ ■ ● ▲ ◼ ● ▲ ■

Introduction

I'll never forget the first children's class I ever taught, and one boy, in particular, cracking an egg. He was seated at a countertop, and, as he'd seen me demonstrate, he cracked the egg on the counter's surface. So far, so good. But then he forgot about the bowl in front of him, and he cradled the cracked egg over his lap. I should have said something, but I didn't.

The boy moved his thumbs inside the crack he'd made in the egg, and began to twist his wrists in opposite directions, trying to pry it open. The shell didn't budge. More forcefully, now, the boy again twisted his wrists, harder and harder until, splat, the egg seemed to implode, and the contents dropped directly into his lap. A pool of egg formed a crater in his apron, like a "flour well" when making homemade pasta. The boy looked up at me. I expected him to be ashamed or humiliated. But he wasn't, because he hadn't known better. He was only confused—he could sense that something just wasn't right. I handed him a towel.

"First time?" I asked.

"Yeah."

I'd taken for granted that everyone knew the basics of cooking. I'd taught children skiing, creative writing, and martial arts, and always knew that the kids were undertaking these activities with little or no prior experience. But, because of my upbringing and all the wonderful time I'd spent with my mother in the kitchen, I'd assumed that all children had a basic understanding of cooking. That, obviously, was not the case, and I was honestly a little relieved.

Until then, I'd had no idea how to go about teaching cooking. I'd seen pictures of children subjected to rows of chairs, and a chef standing in front of the class. I'd watched somewhat luckier kids participate in the cooking process, but they were being taught how to prepare what I call "kid food"—food that was edible but way too easy to prepare—nothing in which they could take any pride. Teaching cooking, I realized, wasn't going to be any different than any other skill I'd had the pleasure of teaching children. Figuratively speaking, we were going to ski the tree trails, write about aliens, and kick each other in the head. We were going to have fun, and we were going to set our goals high.

In one class, called "Stuff Stuffed with Other Stuff," we prepared Inside-Out Spaghetti (baked, whole tomatoes stuffed with spaghetti, fresh basil, onion, pepper, and Parmigiano). In "Global Meatballs," we learned geography and culture through the preparation of Thai Balls, Java Balls, Mexiballs, and Falaf-a-Balls.

The kids were realizing such success in the kitchen that I scheduled a class called "Soufflés Don't Scare Me." This was the true test, and the kids did not let me down. Ham & Cheese Soufflé, Lemon Soufflé, Blueberry Soufflé, Chocolate Soufflé with Vanilla Sauce. Once and for all, together we proved that children's capabilities are only as limitless as we set them up to be.

Real Cooking for Kids is designed to bring similar experiences into your kitchen. While the recipes have known tremendous success in the classroom, it's the approach to preparing them with children that is the key. At Cooking School of Aspen, the techniques required to prepare a recipe are first demonstrated by an adult. After that, however, the children are in charge of the dish. Adults are present to refresh the children's young minds, to clarify and review, but never to intervene. *Real Cooking for Kids* is designed to be used in the same way. The goal, of course, is not just for the soufflés to rise, but also the children's spirits as they watch through glass oven doors their creations take form.

Food for Thought: A Note to Parents

Children, given the opportunity, can and will rise to any occasion. It's up to the adults in their lives to present them with activities that allow them to discover their limitless capabilities.

The focus of this book, then, is not on *easy-to-prepare dishes,* which too often are associated with children's cooking. The recipes in this book are designed to challenge children ages 6 and older, to teach them about cooking, and to inspire them to want to cook more.

Perhaps most importantly, these recipes are designed to provide children with foods they will love—not just to prepare—but also to eat!

You Are What You Eat

"Isn't it important to teach children about nutrition?"

Absolutely not. Who wants to learn about nutrition?

Cooking, presented properly, is about the utilization of raw ingredients. Raw ingredients are healthy and nutritious. It's the processed and pre-prepared foods that are so unhealthy.

When a child learns to enjoy cooking, he or she has already learned to appreciate raw ingredients, and has taken the most important step in nutritional wellness.

Bite Your Tongue: *Adult Supervision vs. Adult Intervention*

It's easy to mistake adult supervision for adult intervention.

Supervision is ensuring that a child is aware of and reminded of the sharpness of the food processor blades. *Intervention* is assembling and disassembling the food processor for the child. *Supervision* is ensuring that a child is at the proper height to flip a pancake safely with a spatula. *Intervention* is flipping the pancakes for the child while the child watches.

You get the picture. How can a child discover his or her limitless capabilities if an adult is always doing, and the child is always watching? Children simply don't have fun watching, and they won't enjoy cooking if they equate it with watching.

Remember: A child will almost always ask for help if he or she can't perform a certain task. Let children ask you for help before you offer it.

I do not suggest, however, that young children do any cutting with any sort of knife: dull, plastic, or sharp. Sharp knives are too dangerous. Dull or plastic knives create bad habits that will prove dangerous when the right time comes for your child to use a knife.

Adult supervision is critical when working with raw meats. Adults must take all necessary precautions to avoid cross-contamination by bacteria.

Putting out a Fire

Do you know how to put out a stovetop fire? It's very simple, and fun to demonstrate to children. Pour about ½ cup of any liquor with a high alcohol content into a saucepan. Heat it on the stovetop. If you're using a gas stove, tilt the pan so the flames "tickle" the inside of the pan. The liquor will light. (If you do not have a gas stove, carefully light the liquor with a long match.)

What shouldn't you do? Do not take the lit pan outside. The fire will grow larger from the increased oxygen supply, and due to forward momentum, the flames will move in the direction of your face. Do not throw water on the fire. The fire will spread in all directions. It is okay to pour flour over the fire, but that's messy.

The easiest way to put out a stove top fire is to cut off its oxygen supply. Simply place another frying pan or large lid over the fire, bottom down or top down—it doesn't matter.

Tips for Cooking with Children

• Children don't like to be shown what to do; they like to do it themselves.

• In order to foster a positive experience, only invite your children into the kitchen with you when you have ample time and little expectation. Cooking for company, for example—when presentation and timeliness are factors—is probably not a great idea.

• Avoid forms of baking that require exactness. It's one thing to bake cookies, where slight mismeasurements don't usually result in disaster, and quite another to make croissants from scratch.

• With just a few exceptions, the recipes here do not require cooking on the stovetop, which is where most accidents occur. For example, the recipe for Bacon 'n' Egg "Muffins" gives children a way to cook bacon and eggs without using the stovetop. For recipes where the stovetop is required, substitute a griddle without a handle, if possible, for a frying pan. Frying pans can tip or fall, while griddles provide better stability.

• Make sure your child can comfortably reach, and has a clear line of sight of, the inside of any pan in which he or she is using a spatula. Using a stool is better than seating your child on the countertop next to the stovetop, which does not provide comfortable access to the pan.

• Do not cook on high heat, to help prevent spattering of hot oil. There's nothing like an oil burn to ruin any chances your child will ever have of enjoying to cook.

• Children won't like cooking if they associate it with having lots of rules. Good habits are easier to instill than attention to rules, and they ensure the same results. The two good habits below don't even have to be verbalized. Just cook this way, always, and so will your children.

> **Good Habit #1:** Read recipes through from start to finish before beginning to cook. You can prevent most mistakes by understanding the process before you start.

> **Good Habit #2:** *Mise en place.* That's French for "things in place" and amounts to all ingredients being prepped and measured prior to any actual cooking being done.

• **Important:** Before you invite children into the kitchen, have all the required chopping and/or slicing done. This way, they will feel an integral part of the cooking process.

• Appliances vs. No Appliances: This is the same as asking, "Should I teach my child to use a computer or a typewriter?" In this day and age, appliances are an integral and fun part of the cooking process.

The Very-Few-Rules Page

1. **Wash your hands** with soap and warm water before you begin cooking. This shows respect for the food and the people who will be enjoying it.

2. **Always have an adult present when you are cooking.** Accidents can happen to anyone. In fact, accidents have been happening to adults for a lot longer than they've been happening to you, which is why it's good to have them around. When it comes to avoiding accidents, adults are the pros!

The Ins and Outs of the Kitchen

Gear

Asian Steamer Basket: There's nothing high-tech about this "appliance." Some things—like the centuries-old bamboo steamer basket—are just impossible to improve upon. It's easier to use than chopsticks, and an addition to your kitchen that your whole family will appreciate.

Baking rack: A mesh rack with short legs to raise it above counter level. Usually used for cooling baked goods.

Baking sheet: A long pan with no sides. The best ones are heavier. Aluminum baking sheets are thin and light, and don't produce good results.

Bowls: Stainless-steel bowls are better than glass, for the simple fact that they don't break. You'll need various sizes: small, medium, and large. Having lots of small bowls on hand is helpful for the practice of *mise en place*. Metal bowls can not be used in the microwave.

Colander: A bowl with holes in it doesn't make much sense, but it works well to drain liquids from solids.

Cutting board: Ingredients which are going to be cut can be placed on a cutting board, made of wood or plastic, to protect your counter top from knife scratches.

Double boiler: Some foods, such as chocolate, will burn if they're placed in a pan over direct heat. You can buy a double boiler, but it's more fun (and less expensive) to make your own. Fill a pot about a third full with water. Place a stainless-steel bowl on the top. If the bottom of the bowl touches the water, the bowl is too deep and you'll need to replace it with a smaller, shallower bowl. Bring the water in the pot to a boil, and place in the bowl the ingredients to be cooked. Adjust heat to a gentle boil.

Frying pan: You'll need a minimum of two, one large and one small—and a third medium-size frying pan is helpful. Frying pans come with nonstick surfaces, which are helpful, but not essential, for cooking foods like eggs, pancakes, French toast, and fish.

Griddle: A large, flat frying pan that is placed directly over one or two burners of your stovetop. We refer to use griddles without handles to reduce the risk of accidents.

Knives: Always ask an adult to help you when it's necessary to use a knife of any kind.

Meat thermometer: Don't put this one under your tongue! Instead, insert it into the center of meats to check for proper doneness. Using one is the safest and most foolproof way to avoid illness from harmful bacteria in undercooked meat.

Muffin tin: A baking pan with individual muffin-size depressions.

Parchment paper: Special cooking paper, not to be confused with waxed paper. Parchment can be placed on the bottom of baking trays for easy clean-up, or food can be wrapped inside parchment for cooking (see Paper Wrapped Chicken on page 19).

Pastry brush: A brush like a wide paintbrush, but used for cooking.

Ramekin: A small ceramic baking dish.

Saucepan: You'll need at least two, and three are helpful: small, large, and medium.

Sheet pan: A long pan with short sides. The best ones are heavier. Aluminum baking sheets are thin and light, and don't produce good results.

Sifter: A strainer for flour that produces lighter, fluffier flour.

Skewer: Wooden or metal rods used for spearing food.

Slotted spoon: This can be a serving spoon, or a kitchen tool, with holes or slots in it to allow liquid to drain through. A spoon with holes is a bit strange, if you ask me, but you'll use it a lot.

Spatula: A small, long-handled, flat "shovel" used to move food around.

Springform pan: A baking pan with removable sides, which makes it very easy to separate the cake from the dish.

Tongs: A big set of "tweezers" used to pick up food.

Whisk: A mixing utensil made of wire loops, used for whipping.

Horsepower

Blender: Life, in general, is more fun with a blender. What would life be like without malts, milkshakes, and smoothies? A kitchen without a blender is like a pool without a diving board. Nothing could be easier to use, either. Throw all the ingredients in, cover, and press a button, any button. Be careful when blending hot liquids—pressure builds up, the top pops off, and scalding liquid sprays everywhere, including all over you. If you're not hurt by the process, you're certain to be utterly humiliated.

Food processor: Slice and dice, pulse and purée—food processors are a blast, and they all have clear sides so you can see what's happening! They're easy to use and a kick to watch, and allow more time for fun and less for work. Read the instructions for your food processor. Essentially, by interchanging the blades, the food processor can do just about any task. They're safe, too, as most won't even turn on unless all the parts are properly assembled. But, as always, be careful! *Never* put your finger or a cooking tool into the processor before unplugging it.

Grill: If you like your neighbors, invite them over for a barbecue. If you don't like your neighbors, grill anyway, but don't invite them over—the delicious smells coming from your yard will drive them crazy.

Ice cream maker: Nothing is as delicious as homemade ice cream, and a good ice cream maker is a cinch to operate. I named mine "Ben." You could name yours "Jerry."

Standing mixer: The workhorse! Using one of these is like holding the reigns of two Clydesdale horses—it will plow through anything with no effort on your part. You can substitute a handheld mixer, which, in many cases, is just as effective.

Sizing It Up

Measuring cups: There are two types: dry and wet. A "dry" measuring cup does not have extra space at the top, and is used for ingredients like flour and sugar. The flat edge of a knife can be used on this style of measuring cup to remove excess ingredient and provide precise measurements. A "wet" measuring cup has extra space at the top, which helps to prevent spilling.

Measuring spoons: There is only one style of measuring spoon for both dry and wet ingredients, but you should have two sets of measuring spoons nonetheless. The flat edge of a knife can be used to level off excess dry ingredient and provide precise measurements.

All Fired Up!

Bake: To cook in an oven using dry heat. This term can be interchanged with *roast*, which also refers to cooking in an oven using dry heat. "Baking" usually refers to cooking treats like muffins and cakes in the oven.

Boil: When bubbles break the surface of a liquid, that liquid is boiling.

Broil: When you turn your oven control to Broil, heat comes from only the top part of the oven. Place foods to broil about 3 to 5 inches from the heat source.

Deep-fry: To cook by submerging food in very hot oil. If not already dry, any ingredients which are going to be deep-fried must be dried by hand by patting with a paper towel or coated with starch or flour. Any moisture that touches hot oil will cause spattering.

Fry: Generally speaking, this term refers to cooking any ingredients in a frying pan on the stovetop. Butter and/or oil are used to keep the ingredients from sticking.

Roast: To cook in an oven using dry heat. This term can be interchanged with *bake*, which also refers to cooking in an oven using dry heat. "Roasting" usually refers to meats and vegetables.

Simmer: To cook gently, with only an occasional bubbling in the saucepan, as opposed to a rapid boil with lots of bubbling going on.

Steam: To cook using the steam from boiling water. You won't want the water boiling too rapidly. Otherwise, it will boil away and you'll be left with no water, which means the food will burn and the bottom of the pot will be scorched.

Stuff Stuffed with Other Stuff

As my mother used to say, "Stuff it."

Inside-Out Spaghetti

Gear

Measuring cups
Spoon
Sheet pan
Parchment paper or aluminum foil
Oven mitts

Ingredients

4 large tomatoes
¹⁄₂ pound cooked spaghetti
A handful of fresh basil leaves,
**   stems removed**
¹⁄₄ cup diced yellow bell pepper
¹⁄₄ cup diced red onion
2 cloves fresh garlic, sliced
Freshly grated Parmesan, preferably
**   Parmigiano-Reggiano**
¹⁄₂ cup chicken stock
Salt
Freshly ground black pepper

Serves 2 to 4

1. Preheat the oven to 425°F.

2. Ask an adult to slice the tops off the tomatoes, just like a Halloween pumpkin. With a spoon, remove and discard the pulp and seeds of the tomatoes, leaving as much as you can of the rest of the tomato's shell.

3. Place the tomatoes on a sheet pan covered with parchment paper or aluminum foil.

4. Inside each tomato, first layer some spaghetti (about 1 inch high), then place on top one basil leaf, followed by a sprinkle of bell pepper and onion. Then add garlic, followed by a layer of Parmesan.

5. Continue to layer in the same order as above, much as you would a lasagna, until the tomatoes are filled.

6. Moisten by spooning a few spoonfuls of stock into each tomato. Sprinkle with Parmesan, and cook in the oven 5 to 10 minutes or just until the sprinkled Parmesan melts.

7. Remove from the oven. Season with salt and pepper, and serve.

Peaches 'n Cream

Gear

Measuring cups
Sheet pan
Parchment paper or aluminum foil
Spoon
Oven mitts

Ingredients

4 large peaches
½ cup whipping cream
Chocolate syrup

Serves 4

1. Preheat the oven to 350°F.

2. Ask an adult to cut a small slice off the bottom of each peach, just enough that each will stand up on its own.

3. Ask an adult to pierce the top of the peach with the tip of a knife, and penetrate, as close to the pit as possible, to the fruit's center. Cut around the pit, and remove it from the peach.

4. Place the peaches on a sheet pan lined with parchment paper or aluminum foil.

5. Fill each peach halfway to the top with cream. Fill the remaining half with chocolate syrup.

6. Place in the oven until peaches are tender but not mushy, 10 to 25 minutes. Cooking times will vary, depending on the ripeness of the peach.

7. Serve in bowls, with a knife, fork, and spoon. You'll see why!

A Year-Round Treat

Normally, I would only suggest purchasing peaches in season. These, however, are going to be roasted, which makes this an ideal dish for enjoying year-round. The roasting both softens and sweetens the peaches.

Cross-Contamination

When I make a really big mistake, I expect the results to be terribly unpleasant. But when I make a small mistake, I hate it when the results are huge. That's how it is with cross-contamination. By definition, cross-contamination occurs anytime a germ moves from a "contaminated" material to a clean material, thereby contaminating the clean material. In the kitchen, foods most likely to cause cross-contamination are raw meats (like pork and beef) and poultry (like chicken and turkey). Cross-contamination typically occurs when a cutting board used to butcher a raw chicken, for example, is not cleaned prior to placing another ingredient on the cutting board—in this case, let's say a tomato. Uncooked chicken germs get on your raw tomato, which you throw into that evening's salad, and the next thing you know, you're moaning in a hospital bed. Here are a few other examples of how cross-contamination occurs in the kitchen:

- **Dirty hands**
- **Dirty dishcloths, towels, aprons**
- **Dirty countertops**
- **Packaging used for raw foods**
- **Pets and pets' bowls**
- **Dirty rinse water and washing bowls**
- **Trash cans**
- **Toys used outside**
- **Dirty kitchen utensils like cutting boards, knives, forks, bowls, and food processors**

Top Ten Things You Can Do to Avoid Cross-Contamination

10. **Rinse fruits and vegetables with clean water before eating them. Remember, fruits and vegetables don't grow in bins in the grocery store. They grow in dirt.**

9. **Don't let foods drip onto other foods in the refrigerator. Duh. Who wants dripping food in the fridge anyway? Like it or not, meats and poultry can drip, and without them you couldn't make meatballs or paper-wrapped chicken.**

8. **Use separate cutting boards and knives for foods you're going to eat raw and foods you're going to eat cooked. Chicken skin on your fresh fruit may not only gross you out; it can make you very sick.**

7. **Wash your hands, including finger-tips, really well with soap and warm water. Dry them well. Wash them again after preparing raw foods such as fish, meat, or poultry. Chefs just might wash their hands even more than doctors!**

6. **A clean kitchen is a healthy kitchen.**

5. **Use lots of hand towels. When one gets dirty, throw it in with the dirty clothes and get a clean one. Wouldn't it be great if you could do the same thing with your shirts?**

4. **Don't cook with your pet. Do something else with your pet. Throw your dog a ball, give your cat a ball of yarn. If your turtle or rabbit insists on joining you in the kitchen, tell them that in some kitchens they could get cooked.**

3. **Don't cook dinner if you're sick. Why would you, anyway, when you could ask for a room-service milkshake?**

2. **Speaking of milkshakes, if you're drinking one while you're working with raw chicken, for example, the raw chicken germs will get on your glass. Be careful!**

1. **And the #1 way to avoid cross-contamination . . . become a famous chef and have someone else do all the prep for you!**

Paper-Wrapped Chicken

Gear

Measuring cups

Measuring spoons

Medium bowl

Medium saucepan

Slotted spoon

Bowl of ice water

Paper towels

Parchment paper, cut into twelve 12-inch squares

Baking sheet

Oven mitts

Ingredients

Marinade (recipe follows)

1 pound skinless, boneless chicken breasts,
    cut into 1$\frac{1}{2}$-inch chunks

$\frac{1}{2}$ head Chinese (Napa) cabbage, cut into 1$\frac{1}{2}$-inch pieces

1 cup bean sprouts

4 scallions, chopped, both white and green parts

Rice (for serving)

Serves 2

1. Add chicken to marinade. Coat well. Marinate in the refrigerator for about 30 minutes.

2. Preheat oven to 400°F.

3. To blanch and shock the cabbage, fill a medium saucepan $\frac{2}{3}$ full of water. Bring to boil, then add cabbage. Cook for 2 minutes. Using a slotted spoon, remove from the boiling water and immediately place into a bowl of ice water. Turn off heat. When cabbage is cool enough to handle, drain and dry on paper towels.

Can I get in trouble with the police for blanching and shocking?

No. "Blanch and shock" means to cook quickly and cool quickly.

Why blanch and shock?

In this case, it's because the cabbage is made up of lots of water. As the cabbage cooks, that water is released, which is good, because otherwise the water would be released inside the paper-wrapped chicken bundle.

The boiling water cooks the cabbage. The ice water stops the cooking process, so the cabbage is not overcooked.

4. On your work surface, place a square of parchment paper in a diamond shape (with one point facing you). In the center of the paper, place 3 pieces of chicken, 5 bean sprouts, a sprinkling of scallion, and 2 pieces of cabbage.

5. Fold the bottom corner of the paper over the filling, a few inches short of the top corner. Fold the right side a couple inches past center, and then the left side just past center, so that one is overlapping the other. Your parchment should kind of look like an open envelope. Fold the bottom to the top to form the "roof of a house." Then fold the roof into the slot you've created! Repeat, and place all 12 packets on a baking sheet. (See the step-by-step diagram below.)

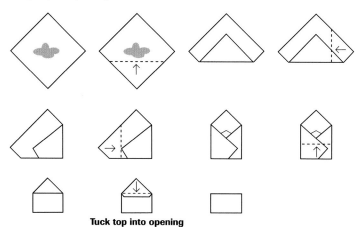

Tuck top into opening

6. Bake in the oven for 5 to 10 minutes. Open the contents of one package to test for doneness before you open all twelve! The center of the chicken should be white. Serve with cooked rice, following directions for cooking on rice package.

Marinade

Ingredients

$\frac{1}{2}$ **cup soy sauce**

1 tablespoon sesame oil (As with all seed and nut oils, this is best kept refrigerated.)

1 tablespoon sugar

1 tablespoon rice vinegar (The label should read *unseasoned*. If it says *seasoned*, leave out the sugar.)

1. Combine all ingredients in a medium plastic or glass bowl.

Potstickers

Gear

- Measuring spoons
- Food processor
- Rubber spatula
- Medium bowl
- Small bowl
- Wok
- Large frying pan
- Tongs or spatula
- 2 or 3 Asian bamboo steamer baskets
- Small saucepan

Ingredients

- 4 ounces ground pork
- 4 ounces whole shrimp, peeled, deveined
- 1 teaspoon peeled, chopped fresh ginger
- 4 cloves fresh garlic
- Handful fresh cilantro, roughly chopped
- 8 leaves Chinese (Napa) cabbage, roughly chopped
- 10 slices of canned, sliced bamboo shoots
- 4 scallions, roughly chopped
- 1 tablespoon Sambal Oelek (or your own favorite chili sauce; Sambal Oelek is mine!)
- 1 tablespoon soy sauce
- About 40 wonton wraps
- 2 to 3 tablespoons cooking oil
- Sweet, Sour, Hot, and Salty Dipping Sauce (recipe follows)

Serves 4

Be Creative!

Potstickers can be filled with any variety of your favorite fillings. Try the recipe with steak, chicken, shrimp, or pork and see which you prefer!

1. Combine all the ingredients, except the wonton wraps and cooking oil, in a food processor. Pulse until well combined, stopping if necessary to scrape the ingredients away from the sides of the processor and into the center. (A rubber spatula works best for this.)

2. Unplug the food processor. With a rubber spatula, remove the filling, and place in a medium bowl.

3. Spread out ten wonton wraps at a time on your work surface, along with a small bowl of warm water.

4. Wet the tip of one finger, and run it across the edges of each wonton, only slightly wetting the wonton. (Too much water will make the wonton sticky!)

5. Place a small amount of filling (about 1 heaping tablespoon) in the center of each wonton wrap. Gather the wrap around the filling, and pinch all 4 corners at the top to seal.

6. Fill a wok with 2 to 3 inches of water, and place over high heat until the water comes to a boil. Heat a large frying pan and cover the bottom with cooking oil. When oil is hot, add the wontons. Add as many as you can work with easily, but not so many that they touch each other. You may have to make more than one batch. When the bottoms are a crispy golden brown, use tongs or a spatula to remove. You want to brown only one side. Browning happens quickly, so be ready.

7. Place potstickers in Asian steamer baskets, crispy-side down, and set the basket on the wok over the boiling water. Cover and steam the potstickers for about 5 minutes. To check for doneness, remove one potsticker, and cut into it. The meat should turn from pink to white when it's done. If one is done, they're all done, as long as equal amounts of filling were put into each potsticker. Serve with Sweet, Sour, Hot, and Salty Dipping Sauce.

Sweet, Sour, Hot, and Salty Dipping Sauce

Ingredients

¼ cup unseasoned rice vinegar

¼ cup soy sauce

¼ cup water

¼ cup sugar

2 tablespoons Thai fish sauce

3 cloves fresh garlic, thinly sliced

¼ jalapeño chile

Juice of 1 fresh lime

3 leaves of fresh basil, torn

1. In a small saucepan, combine all the ingredients and heat to boiling. When sauce reaches a boil, remove from heat, and let cool to room temperature.

2. Remove jalapeño chile, and serve in small dipping bowls with Potstickers (see recipe on page 21).

8 servings

● ▲ ■ ● ▲ ■ ● ▲ ■ ●

Sweet, Sour, Salty, Bitter

Before you make this dish, set out the following ingredients in their own small bowls: rice vinegar or lime juice, soy sauce, sugar, and a small piece of the rind of the lime.

Taste each one to detect sour, salty, sweet, and bitter.

What do our tongues do?

Not much, really, when it comes to tasting. It's our noses that do all the work. All our tongues can do is detect sweet, sour, bitter, and salty. When you bite into an orange, for example, all your tongue tells your brain is that something sweet is in your mouth. It's your nose that knows it's orangey.

Likewise, when you bite into a lemon, all your tongue does is tell your brain that something sour is in your mouth. Your nose knows it's lemony.

What makes food interesting is a balance of sweet, sour, bitter, and salty. The more of those elements you can incorporate into a dish, the more interesting and flavorful it will be.

A Hug and a Kiss

Gear

Rolling pin
3-inch biscuit cutter (or a glass with a 3-inch diameter)
Parchment paper
Baking sheet
Oven mitts
Cooling rack
Tea ball (optional)
Measuring cups
Measuring spoons
Sifter
Medium bowl
Standing mixer, or hand-held mixer and bowl
Plastic wrap

Ingredients

Sugar Cookie Dough (recipe follows)
24 unwrapped chocolate kisses (or a whole bag if you want to nibble!)
Powdered sugar (optional)

Makes 24 cookies

● ▲ ■ ● ▲ ■ ● ▲ ■ ● ▲ ■ ● ▲ ■ ● ▲ ■ ● ▲ ■ ● ▲

1. Preheat the oven to 350°F.

2. Use a rolling pin to roll out the cookie dough to about ⅛-inch thick.

3. Using a 3-inch biscuit cutter (or a glass with an approximately 3-inch diameter), cut out circles of dough.

4. Place a kiss in the center of each dough circle.

5. Carefully gather the dough around each kiss, and pinch at the top to seal.

6. Transfer each one to a parchment paper-lined baking sheet. Leave plenty of room in between cookies—don't crowd them on the pan. Bake 8 to 10 minutes until the cookies are golden. Remove from the oven and cool on the pan for 5 minutes before moving to a cooling rack. Sprinkle with powdered sugar. (A tea ball or a sieve works great for this!). Enjoy!

Sugar Cookie Dough

Ingredients

2 cups all-purpose flour
¼ teaspoon salt
½ teaspoon baking powder
½ cup (1 stick) unsalted butter,
softened
1 cup sugar
1 egg
2 tablespoons milk
½ teaspoon vanilla extract

Makes 24 (2 dozen)

1. Sift together the flour, salt, and baking powder in a medium bowl.

2. Cream the butter and sugar in the mixer bowl. Add the egg, milk, and vanilla, and thoroughly mix.

3. Add the dry ingredients a little bit at a time, and mix until well blended. Unplug the mixer, clean the beaters with your fingers or a spatula, and remove the bowl.

4. Remove the dough from the bowl and place it on a sheet of plastic wrap. Press it into a big pancake that is about ¾-inch thick. Chill for at least two hours in the refrigerator.

Make a
Pig of Yourself

You are what you eat.

Bacon, Lettuce & Tomato Sandwich

Gear

Sheet pan
Metal spatula
Plate
Paper towels
Toaster

Ingredients

6 strips of bacon
2 tomato slices
2 slices of your favorite bread
Homemade Mayonnaise (recipe follows)
3 lettuce leaves

Serves 1

● ▲ ■ ● ▲ ■ ● ▲ ■ ● ▲ ■ ● ▲ ■ ● ▲ ■ ● ▲ ■ ● ▲

1. Preheat oven to 350°F. Leaving a bit of space between each strip, place bacon on a sheet pan. Bake for 15-20 minutes. Remove sheet pan from oven, and place bacon on a plate covered with paper towels to soak up the grease.

2. Ask an adult to slice the tomato with a serrated knife.

3. Toast your favorite bread. Slather both slices with Homemade Mayonnaise. On one slice, layer bacon, then tomatoes, then top with lettuce. Cover with the second slice of bread. Slice in half, and serve with pickles and potato chips.

Question

Where does mayonnaise come from, anyway?
See if you can answer this question before looking at the ingredients on the next page.

Homemade Mayonnaise

Gear

Measuring spoons
Measuring cup
Blender or food processor

Ingredients

1 egg (*see Note to Parents, below)
¼ teaspoon cayenne
½ teaspoon dry mustard
Salt
White pepper
1½ tablespoons rice vinegar
½ tablespoon lemon juice
1 cup canola or other neutral oil,
    or a combination,
    in an easy-to-pour container

Makes 1 cup

▲ ■ ● ▲ ■ ● ▲ ■ ● ▲

1. In the container of a blender or food processor, combine the egg, cayenne, mustard, salt, pepper, vinegar, lemon juice, and ¼ cup of the oil. Turn on the machine and, with it running, pour in the remaining oil in a very slow, very thin, steady stream.

2. When you've added about half the oil, the mixture will thicken; at this point, you can begin adding the oil just a little faster. Taste, and add salt if necessary. Serve immediately or store in the refrigerator for up to a week.

*Note to Parents: Uncooked eggs can harbor salmonella bacteria, a possible source of food poisoning. To lessen the risk, purchase pasteurized eggs, now available at most supermarkets.

Question: Why choose white pepper instead of black?

Answer: The white pepper is used because mayonnaise would look funny with black specks in it.

Emulsifiers

Try this: Pour a pool of oil onto a white plate. Squeeze some lemon juice, or pour some vinegar, into the oil. Stir them—try to combine them.

    Impossible, right?

    You can't mix oil with an acid (like vinegar or lemon juice), any more than you can oil and water.

    That is, unless you have an emulsifier, an ingredient that allows oils and acids to combine. Without an emulsifier, it would have been impossible to combine the oil with the lemon juice and vinegar to make the mayonnaise.

    You only need one emulsifier, but it just so happens, the mayonnaise recipe contains two. What are they?

Answer: Mustard, Egg

Asian-Style Baby Back Ribs

Gear

Measuring cups

Measuring spoons

Baking dish with sides 2 to 3 inches high

Bowl

Plastic container

Sheet pan

Parchment paper

Aluminum foil

Wire rack

Oven mitts

Pastry brush

Ingredients

**3 to 4 pounds baby back ribs, chopped
in half lengthwise (optional) by your butcher**

Marinade (recipe follows)

$\frac{1}{2}$ cup honey

Serves 4

■ ● ▲ ■ ● ▲ ■ ● ▲ ■

1. Preheat the oven 325°F.

2. Rinse the ribs under running water, and place bone side down in a high-sided baking dish. Add about half an inch of water, seal tightly with aluminum foil, and place in the oven for about 2 hours. This slow steaming makes the ribs tender. Remove from the oven and allow the ribs to cool enough that you can handle them. Ask an adult to help you discard the fat from the pan.

3. Ask an adult to slice the ribs between the bones into segments of two ribs each. Place the ribs in a plastic container. Pour the marinade over the ribs, taking care to coat them totally. Cover with a lid or plastic wrap and place in the refrigerator. Marinate at least 6 hours or overnight.

2. Preheat oven to 450°F. Cover a sheet pan with parchment paper or aluminum foil.

3. Remove ribs from marinade and place them on a wire rack. Discard marinade.

4. Place ribs on foil-lined sheet pan. Place in oven, and cook for about 5 minutes.

5. Meanwhile, in a microwave-safe container, heat honey in the microwave for 30 seconds on high. Remove the ribs from the oven, and brush the honey on the ribs with a pastry brush, just like you would paint a picket fence. Return to oven for about 5 minutes more, until ribs are browned and crispy.

Marinade

Ingredients

- $\frac{1}{4}$ cup chopped garlic
- $\frac{1}{2}$ tablespoon fresh peeled, chopped ginger
- $\frac{1}{4}$ cup soy sauce
- 1 tablespoon sesame oil
- 2 teaspoons salt
- 2 tablespoons sugar
- 3 tablespoons hoisin sauce

1. In a bowl, combine the marinade ingredients.

It's ok to marinate beef, chicken, or pork overnight, but not seafood. Twenty to thirty minutes is plenty of time to marinate most seafood.

Bacon 'N' Egg "Muffins"

Gear

Muffin tin

Oven mitts

2 forks

Measuring spoons

Spoon

Ingredients

6 strips of bacon

6 eggs

¼ cup (½ stick) melted butter

Salt

Freshly ground black pepper

Chili powder

Makes 6 "Muffins"

1. Preheat oven to 350°F.

2. Wrap the bacon slices around the insides but not the bottoms of six individual muffin cups. Wash your hands well with lots of soap and warm water after you handle the bacon.

3. Place the muffin tin in the oven, and bake for 15 to 20 minutes or until the bacon is cooked through and just short of crispy. Remove from the oven.

4. The bacon should have cooked in the shape of a cup with no bottom. It may have shrunk and pulled away from the sides of the muffin molds. If necessary, use two forks to spread apart the bacon, pushing it back up against the sides of the muffin cups.

5. Drop a whole egg into each of the bacon "cups." Try not to let the yolk break, but if it does, it's okay. Top each with 1 tablespoon of melted butter.

6. Sprinkle each Bacon 'N' Egg "Muffin" with salt, pepper, and a bit of chili powder, then place the muffin tin back into the oven and cook until the eggs are done—about 5 minutes, just a few more minutes once they have turned white.

7. Remove from the oven, and ask an adult to slide a dinner knife around the edge of the Bacon 'N' Egg Muffins, loosening them from the sides of the muffin tin. With a spoon, lift the Bacon 'N' Egg Muffins onto a plate. Most of the bacon grease and butter should stay behind in the muffin cups. Serve with buttered toast.

Mudslides

Gear
Blender
Ice cream scoop or spoon

Ingredients
5 scoops of vanilla ice cream
1 scoop of cream of coconut
2 handfuls ice
2 squeezes chocolate syrup
Milk to consistency

Serves 4

■ ● ▲ ■ ● ▲ ■ ●

1. Combine all ingredients except milk in blender. Blend until smooth. Add milk a little at a time to help make it smooth enough to drink.

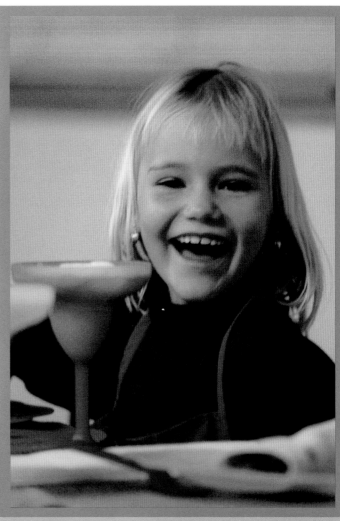

Cream of Coconut can be found in the grocery store near Margarita and Piña Colada mixes.

Eggs

Without eggs, there would be little purpose for kitchens.

In these recipes, you'll see how eggs are used not just in baking, but as food glue, glazes, and as leaveners to create millions of little bubbles to help foods rise like hot air balloons.

Eggs are the magic in so many dishes. In fact, this year, Americans will eat an average of 250 eggs each.

Lemon-Poppyseed Pancakes

Gear

Measuring spoons
Measuring cups
Juicer
Whisk
2 large bowls
1 small bowl
Spoon
Large frying pan or griddle
Spatula

Ingredients

1 cup all-purpose flour
1 teaspoon sugar
1/2 teaspoon salt
3/4 teaspoon double-acting baking powder
1/2 teaspoon baking soda
1 egg
1 cup buttermilk
Juice of one lemon, no seeds
1/4 cup poppyseeds
Butter (for serving)
Maple syrup (for serving)

Serves 2 to 4

■ ● ▲ ■ ● ▲ ■ ● ▲

1. With a whisk, combine the dry ingredients in a large bowl.

2. Separate the egg by first cracking the shell, then gently dropping the whole egg close to the bottom of a small bowl without breaking the yolk. Remove any shell. With your fingers in the shape of a claw, gently cradle the yolk of the egg, and lift it out of the bowl. Hold it above the bowl, with your fingers spread apart, allowing the clear part (called the *white*) of the egg to drip back into the bowl. When all the white has dripped into the bowl, drop the yolk into a large bowl.

3. With a whisk, whip egg white until frothy, about 1 minute.

4. Add the frothy egg white to the bowl with the yolk. Stir in the buttermilk and lemon juice.

5. Add the dry ingredients to the wet ingredients. Mix them together with a spoon, but do not over-stir. Stir in the poppyseeds. It's okay if the batter is a little lumpy.

6. Heat the griddle or large frying pan over medium heat. Use a little butter in the bottom of the pan to keep the pancakes from sticking. For each pancake, pour between 1/4 to 1/2 cup of batter onto the griddle or frying pan. Flip when the pancakes begin to bubble on the top and the bottom is golden brown. Don't rush the flipping—if you flip the pancakes too soon, you'll just end up with a big mess. Serve with butter and maple syrup.

This is a great recipe to practice *mise en place*, a French term meaning that all ingredients have been prepared (chopped, measured, cleaned) prior to any actual cooking. *Mise en place* makes cooking fun. Failure to practice *mise en place* can result in brief periods of misery. Before you start to cook, have your ingredients measured into small bowls.

Wet or Dry?

In a lot of baking, recipes will ask you to combine dry ingredients and wet ingredients separately. Then the recipe will ask you to combine the wet with the dry.

Question: In this recipe, which ingredients are dry? Which are wet?

Answer:
Dry: flour, sugar, salt, baking powder, baking soda
Wet: egg, buttermilk, lemon juice

Strawberry Cheesecake Ice Cream

Gear

Measuring cups

Measuring spoons

Small saucepan

Spoon

Whisk

Ice cream maker

Food processor

9- to 12-inch springform pan

Standing mixer

Oven mitts

Aluminum foil

Two Recipes in One

The fun part about this recipe is that you can make the cheesecake one day, and the strawberry cheesecake ice cream the next! Cheesecake is always much, much better the second day anyway!

Ingredients

3 cups heavy (whipping) cream

¾ cup sugar

⅛ teaspoon salt

1 vanilla bean (or 4 teaspoons vanilla extract)

1 cup milk

One wedge of a Strawberry Cheesecake (recipe follows)

Serves a bunch!

● ▲ ■ ● ▲ ■ ● ▲ ■ ● ▲ ■ ● ▲ ■ ● ▲ ■ ● ▲ ■ ● ▲

1. Measure 1 cup of the cream and put it in a small saucepan. Put the remaining 2 cups of the cream in the refrigerator—you won't need it for a while. Over low heat, slowly heat 1 cup of the cream, taking care not to bring it to a boil. When the cream is hot, stir in the sugar and the salt.

2. Ask an adult to use a sharp knife to slice lengthwise through the skin of the vanilla bean. Spread the bean open, and with the tip of a spoon, scrape inside of each half of the bean, collecting the tiny seeds inside, leaving the bean to resemble the shape of a canoe. Discard the vanilla bean skin. Add the insides of the vanilla bean to the cream mixture, and stir to combine. If you do not have access to vanilla beans, substitute 4 teaspoons of vanilla extract.

3. Place mixture in the refrigerator, and chill until cold, for at least a few hours.

4. With a whisk, combine the remaining 2 cups of cream, 1 cup of milk, and the vanilla cream mixture. Place in ice cream maker with large chunks of the cheesecake and the ice cream mix. (You'll need only one wedge of the cheesecake. Enjoy the rest for a separate dessert, or serve some to an adult with a cup of coffee.) Churn according to your ice cream maker's instructions.

Strawberry Cheesecake

Ingredients

- 1 9-ounce package Nabisco Famous Chocolate Wafer cookies, graham crackers, or chocolate grahams
- 8 tablespoons (1 stick) butter, roughly chopped, room temperature
- 1 tablespoon sugar
- 1 pound cream cheese
- 1 large egg, lightly beaten
- 1/3 cup sugar
- 1/2 teaspoon vanilla extract
- 1 tablespoon cornstarch
- 1/2 cup sour cream
- 8 ounces fresh strawberries, cleaned, stemmed and sliced in half

Makes 1 cheesecake

1. Break up half the cookies (about 4½ ounces), and place in a food processor, along with 6 tablespoons of the butter and 1 tablespoon of sugar. (The remaining cookies are for you to nibble on!) You can substitute graham crackers or chocolate grahams if you can't find Famous Chocolate Wafers. Pulse until mixture passes the Pinch Perfect Test (see page 41), but always remember to unplug the food processor before putting your fingers in it! If you're using graham crackers or chocolate grahams, you might need to add more butter than is called for in the ingredients.

2. Use the remaining butter to grease the bottom and sides of a 9- to 12-inch spring-form pan and press crust evenly onto bottom.

3. Preheat the oven to 350°F.

4. In the bowl of a standing mixer, using the whip attachment, beat together the cream cheese, egg, and 1/3 cup sugar until smooth and light.

5. Beat in the vanilla and cornstarch, taking care not to overmix. Beat in the sour cream. Turn off the mixer. Add the strawberries, and stir gently at low speed or by hand. Unplug the mixer and clean the beaters with your fingers or a rubber spatula.

6. Pour the mixture over the crust, and bake for 50 to 70 minutes in the preheated oven. Cheesecakes require the jiggle test to see if they're done. Remove the cheesecake from the oven, and jiggle it gently. If it's too jiggly, the cheesecake needs to be put back. If it jiggles just slightly, it's done, as it will continue to cook even after you remove it from the oven. If the top gets too brown but still needs more baking, loosely place the foil over the top of the pan. Don't wrap or seal the foil over the cake.

7. Allow the cheesecake to cool to room temperature. Cover it very gently with foil, and place in the refrigerator. This is Day 1. Don't eat or use in ice cream until Day 2. To remove from springform pan, ask an adult to slide a dinner knife between the cake and the pan to separate the cake from the pan, then remove the pan's sides.

The Pinch-Perfect Test

To determine whether the crust is of the right consistency, pinch a little bit of crust dough. If it stays pinched, it's perfect. If it falls apart, add some more butter, and pulse until well combined. Retest using the pinch method. Add butter until your dough is pinch-perfect!

Chocolate Soufflé with Vanilla Sauce

Gear

Paper towel

8 ramekins

3 medium bowls

Sheet pan

Double boiler (you can make your own!)

Wooden or plastic spoon

Whisk

Standing mixer or hand mixer

Rubber spatula

Spoon

Ingredients

¼ cup butter

Medium-size bowl of sugar

1 cup semi-sweet chocolate chips or chunks

3 tablespoons heavy cream

1 tablespoon all-purpose flour

1 tablespoon vanilla extract

8 eggs, room temperature

2 scoops of your favorite vanilla ice cream, melted, room temperature

Serves 8

● ▲ ■ ● ▲ ■ ● ▲ ■ ● ▲ ■ ● ▲ ■ ● ▲ ■ ● ▲ ■ ● ▲ ■ ● ▲

1. Take a pat of butter and use a paper towel to spread it all over the inside of a ramekin to form a light coating. Dip a ramekin in the bowl of sugar, filling it with several tablespoons of sugar. Hold the ramekin at an angle above the bowl and spin the ramekin so that the sugar sticks to the butter and lines the sides and bottom of the ramekin. Pour out the remaining sugar into the bowl, and repeat with remaining ramekins. Place the ramekins on a sheet pan and set aside.

2. In the bowl of the double boiler (see page 43), melt the chocolate chips with the cream, flour, and vanilla, stirring occasionally, until the chocolate melts and the mixture is smooth. Keep the double boiler on a low heat until you are ready to use the chocolate mixture.

3. Preheat the oven to 375°F.

4. Separate six of the eggs by gently dropping them one at a time into a medium bowl, taking care not to let the yolks break. (If a yolk breaks, you'll have to start over, but that's okay. Save those eggs for tomorrow's breakfast, and start again with a clean bowl.) With your fingers in the shape of a claw, gently cradle the yolk of one

egg at a time, and lift it out of the bowl. Hold it above the bowl, with your fingers spread apart, allowing the clear part (called the *white*) of the egg to drip back into the bowl. When all the white has dripped into the bowl, drop the yolk into a separate, medium-size bowl. Repeat until you have 6 whites and 5 yolks. (You'll have to throw away one yolk.)

5. Combine the remaining 2 whole eggs with the yolks. While whisking, spoon several tablespoons of hot chocolate mixture into the egg and yolk mixture. This is called *tempering*. It is important to add the hot mixture slowly so that you don't wind up cooking the eggs—there's nothing grosser than scrambled eggs in your chocolate soufflé!

6. When half the chocolate mixture has been added to the eggs, whisk the rest of the yolk mixture into the chocolate mixture. Set aside.

7. In the bowl of a mixer, beat the egg whites until stiff peaks form. Unplug the mixer and remove the bowl.

8. Use a rubber spatula to gently fold a quarter of the beaten whites into the warm chocolate mixture to lighten it. Then fold in the remaining egg whites until the mixture is all the same color.

9. Working quickly (but don't rush), spoon the mixture into the prepared ramekins, filling to about $1/2$-inch from the top. Bake the soufflés on a sheet pan in the middle of the oven until well-puffed, about 10 to 15 minutes.

10. Remove from the oven. Use a spoon to make a cut in the top of each soufflé, and add some melted vanilla ice cream. Take care, as the ramekins are very hot! Enjoy, and be proud of your creation.

How to Make a Double Boiler

If you don't already have one, you can fashion a double boiler by placing a metal bowl over a saucepan about $1/3$ full of water. Bring the water to a boil, and you have a home made double boiler.

The steam from the boiling water heats the metal bowl, which gently heats the contents of the metal bowl. If the boiling water is touching the bottom of the bowl, you'll need to use a smaller or shallower bowl.

How Is a Soufflé Like a Hot Air Balloon?

See if you can answer this question: Why do the egg whites look different after having been beaten? What's inside them now that wasn't before?

The answer: Air.

A soufflé is kind of like a balloon. What happens when you're too rough on a balloon? It pops, and all the air is released. Just like a balloon, a soufflé is full of air bubbles inside the beaten egg whites. When the air inside the soufflé warms from the oven, the bubbles expand and the soufflé rises, just like a hot air balloon.

Katie's Bear Bread

Gear

- Measuring cups
- Measuring spoons
- 2 large bowls
- Plastic wrap
- Baking sheet
- Pastry brush
- Aluminum foil
- Oven mitts
- Spatula
- Wire rack

Ingredients

- 1 package active dry yeast
- $\frac{1}{3}$ cup sugar
- $\frac{1}{4}$ cup warm water (105 to 110°F on a kitchen thermometer)*
- 2 eggs
- 4 tablespoons ($\frac{1}{2}$ stick) butter, melted
- $\frac{1}{4}$ cup milk, room temperature
- 1 tablespoon vanilla extract
- $\frac{1}{2}$ teaspoon salt
- 1 level tablespoon fresh rosemary, minced, no stems
- $2\frac{1}{2}$ to 3 cups all-purpose flour
- Oil or butter
- Egg glaze (see note on page 45)

Makes 5 to 6 bears, 6 inches in length

▲ ■ ● ▲ ■ ● ▲ ■ ● ▲

1. In a large bowl, sprinkle the yeast and sugar into the warm water.* Gently stir until the yeast and sugar have dissolved, then allow the mixture to rest for at least 4 minutes to make sure the yeast is alive and active.

2. When the yeast has foamed up (if the yeast does not foam, you'll need to purchase new yeast), add the eggs, butter, milk, vanilla, salt, and rosemary. Stir until thoroughly mixed.

*This temperature is important, because if the water is too hot, it kills the yeast. If the water is too cold, the yeast will not be activated.

3. Stir in $2\frac{1}{2}$ cups flour.

4. Place the dough onto a floured work surface and knead—adding more flour one tablespoon at a time as necessary—until smooth, about 6 to 7 minutes. See note on kneading on page 45. Finish by forming the dough into a ball.

5. With oil or butter, grease the inside of a large bowl. Place the ball of dough in it, turning to coat the dough. Cover with plastic wrap, and leave in a warm place to rise. (A microwave where you have just heated one cup of water to boiling is a perfect place to let your bread rise.) Allow to rise for about $1\frac{1}{2}$ hours.

6. With lightly floured hands, turn the dough out, and tear pieces to form each part of a bear, starting with the body. Keep the dough you are not working with covered, so that it will not dry out.

7. Preheat the oven to 350°F.

8. Shape each part of the animal by rolling the dough into a ball, then flattening it with the palm of your hand. Place the body on a greased baking sheet. To attach the rest of the bear's parts, use the egg glaze (see page 45) as glue, and gently pinch pieces together. Repeat with remaining dough.

9. With a pastry brush, paint the surface with the egg glaze. You can use two Cheerios, raisins, or whatever you like as eyes. Place in the oven to bake, for about 15 to 20 minutes. Cooking times will vary with size of your bears and altitude, so watch carefully. If you see that some parts of your bears are cooking more quickly than others, ask an adult to gently cover those parts with pieces of aluminum foil.

10. When the bears are golden, use a spatula to remove them, and allow to cool on a wire rack for about 30 minutes.

Before You Knead, Read!

Kneading is a blast and works like this:

With floured hands, fold the dough in half, from bottom to top. Use your palms to press the dough firmly from top to bottom one time. Rotate the dough ¼ turn, fold in half from top to bottom, and press with the palms of your hands. Repeat.

Using Eggs as a Glaze

Katie is a Cooking School of Aspen children's instructor and a brilliant baker. She has great tips for using eggs as a glaze: "For this recipe, I like to use a glaze with 1 egg yolk whisked with 1 teaspoon water to produce a rich golden color. You can also use just 1 egg white and 1 teaspoon water if you want a transparent glaze without a golden color."

B'egged Potato

Gear

- Measuring cups
- Measuring spoons
- Spoon
- Fork
- Large bowl
- Whisk
- 2 large frying pans or griddles
- Plastic or wooden spoon
- Sheet pan
- Oven mitts
- Plate
- Paper towels
- Baking sheet
- Parchment paper or aluminum foil

Ingredients

- 2 large, cooked baked potatoes
- 6 eggs
- 2 tablespoons butter
- Cooking oil
- 8 slices of bacon
- 2 cups grated cheddar cheese

Serves 4

Leftover baked potatoes work best for this dish!

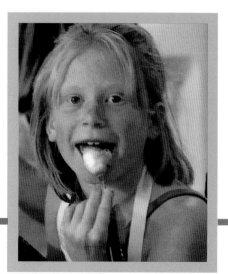

1. Ask an adult to slice two baked potatoes in half. With a spoon, scoop out the flesh of each potato half, taking care to leave approximately ¼-inch of "skin."

2. Use a fork to break up the removed flesh of each potato to form small to medium-size chunks. Set aside.

3. Preheat oven to 350°F.

4. In a large bowl, beat the eggs with a whisk or fork. Heat a large frying pan or griddle over medium heat. Add about 2 tablespoons of butter, and when the butter is melted, pour the eggs into the pan. Scramble the eggs by gently moving them around with a plastic or wooden spoon so that the uncooked eggs touch the bottom of the pan. Continue stirring until they are cooked through but still moist, about 5 minutes. Remove from the stovetop. Set aside.

5. Leaving a bit of space between each strip, place bacon on a sheet pan. Bake for 15 to 20 minutes. Remove sheet pan from oven, and place bacon on a plate covered with paper towels to soak up the grease. When bacon is cool, break it up into large bits.

6. In another large frying pan, heat enough cooking oil to coat the bottom of the pan. Add the potatoes, and cook until browned, 5 to 7 minutes. (Try not to move the potatoes around too much: that's the secret to sucessful browning.)

7. When the potatoes are done, turn off the heat and add the eggs, bacon, and half of the cheese. Combine, but do not overstir.

8. Place the potato skins on a baking sheet lined with parchment paper or aluminum foil.

9. Spoon the egg mixture into the potato halves. Sprinkle the remaining cheese over the potatoes, and bake in the oven until cheese is melted, 10 to 15 minutes.

Global Meatballs

Meat Your Maker...

Every kid around the world has a meatball to call his or her own.

Here are just a few!

What do the following recipes have in common? The answers to this question are the key to making great meatballs.

If meatballs could fly, the good ones would glide through the air like a wiffle ball—the bad ones would soar like a baseball. That's because the good ones have an ingredient like bread, daal, or masa harina to make them lighter than meat on its own. Good meatballs also have a binder, a beaten egg, to keep them from falling apart.

What are some of the differences between the following recipes? The answers to this question are the keys to understanding the ingredients of various cultures.

The Java Balls use cumin, soy sauce, ginger, coconut milk, lemongrass, cinnamon, curry, and peanuts—the ingredients of Indonesia!

The Stuffed Meatballs use lamb instead of beef, plus daal, ginger, chile, cardamom, clove, cinnamon, coriander, coconut, and mint—the ingredients of India!

The Greek Balls use oregano, mint, lemon, tomato, cucumber, onion, and yogurt—the ingredients of Greece!

The Mexiballs use scallions, tomatoes, chiles, garlic, tortillas, masa harina, and cilantro—the ingredients of Mexico!

Falaf-A-Balls use chickpeas, lemon, parsley, tomato, and yogurt—the ingredients of the Middle East!

What other types of meatballs can you think of?

Java Balls (Indonesian-style)

Gear

Measuring cups
Measuring spoons
Meat pounder (optional)
Medium saucepan
Spoon
Food processor
Rubber spatula
Sheet pan
Parchment paper or aluminum foil
Oven mitts
Medium saucepan
Strainer

Ingredients

2 stalks lemongrass, the top ⅔ (the thin part)
discarded (optional)
1 (13.5-ounce) can coconut milk
3-inch cinnamon stick
2 tablespoons sugar
1 tablespoon salt
1 tablespoon curry powder
½ cup bread crumbs
¼ cup all-purpose flour
3 cloves fresh garlic, roughly chopped
½ teaspoon ground cumin
1 tablespoon soy sauce
½ teaspoon pepper
1 tablespoon finely chopped peeled fresh ginger
1 egg
1 pound ground beef
3 packages of ramen noodles
½ cup dry roasted, salted peanuts (for serving)
2 scallions, root end removed, finely chopped

Serves 4 to 6

1. Pound the lemongrass with the bumpy side of a meat pounder (or anything that will mash it up).

2. In a medium saucepan, combine the contents of 1 can of coconut milk with the lemongrass, cinnamon stick, sugar, salt, and curry powder. Bring to a boil, then reduce heat to a simmer, and cook for 15 minutes.

3. Preheat oven to 450°F.

4. Meanwhile, in a food processor, combine and process the bread crumbs, flour, garlic, cumin, soy sauce, pepper, ginger, and the egg. Add ground beef, and process until combined but not over-processed, stopping if necessary to scrape the ingredients away from the sides of the processor and into the center. (A rubber spatula works best for this.)

5. Unplug the food processor, remove the blade, and form the mixture into small meatballs. To shape into perfect balls, roll each meatball between both palms. The actual size doesn't matter, as long as they're all the same size. This way, they will all cook evenly.

6. Place the meatballs on a sheet pan lined with parchment paper or aluminum foil, and bake in oven until browned. Large meatballs take longer to cook than small meatballs. To test for doneness, cut into one meatball. There should be no red color left in the meat.

7. Cook ramen noodles according to package directions. Do not add seasoning packets. Strain noodles.

8. Place noodles in the bottom of four bowls. Remove the cinnamon stick and lemongrass from the sauce. Spoon meatballs and sauce over noodles. Serve with peanuts and scallions.

Stuffed Meatballs (Indian-style)

Gear

Measuring cups

Measuring spoons

Small saucepan

Colander

Food processor

Rubber spatula

Sheet pan

Parchment paper or aluminum foil

Oven mitts

Ingredients

⅓ cup daal (split peas)

2 tablespoons onion, roughly chopped

1 teaspoon peeled, chopped fresh ginger

½ jalapeño chile, stemmed and seeded, roughly chopped

4 whole cardamom pods, split, seeds removed

1 teaspoon ground clove

1 teaspoon ground cinnamon

1 teaspoon ground coriander

1 teaspoon ground cumin

1½ teaspoons salt

¼ cup flaked coconut (sweetened or unsweetened)

1 egg

¾ pound ground lamb

Fresh mint leaves

Fresh cilantro leaves

Raisins

Rice (for serving)

Plain yogurt (for serving)

Serves 4

● ▲ ■ ● ▲ ■ ● ▲ ■ ● ▲ ■ ● ▲ ■ ● ▲ ■ ● ▲ ■ ● ▲

If you wet your hands while you're rolling meatballs, it's a much less sticky process!

1. Rinse the daal, then place in a small saucepan. Add 3 cups of water, and bring to a boil. Reduce heat to low, and cook until the daal are tender but not mushy, at least 20 minutes. Remove the daal, and place in a colander to drain and dry.

2. Preheat oven to 350°F.

3. In the food processor, combine and process the daal, onion, ginger, jalapeño, cardamom, clove, cinnamon, coriander, cumin, salt, coconut, and egg. Add lamb, and process until combined, stopping if necessary to scrape the ingredients away from the sides of the processor and into the center. (A rubber spatula works best for this.) Unplug the food processor, remove blade, and form mixture into meatballs about 2 inches in diameter. To shape into perfect balls, roll each meatball between both palms.

4. Using the palm of your hand, flatten each meatball, then make a small indentation in the center with your thumb. In the indentation, place three small mint leaves, three cilantro leaves and three raisins. Wrap meat around filling, and shape back into meatballs.

5. Place meatballs on a sheet pan lined with parchment paper or aluminum foil, and bake until cooked through, about 20 minutes.

6. Serve over rice, preferably basmati, and top with a dollop of plain room-temperature yogurt.

Peeling Ginger

It's easiest to peel ginger with the side of a spoon.

Greek Balls

Gear

- **Measuring cup**
- **Measuring spoons**
- **Food processor**
- **Rubber spatula**
- **Sheet pan**
- **Parchment paper or aluminum foil**
- **Oven mitts**
- **Vegetable peeler**
- **Spoon**
- **Small bowl**

Ingredients

- **¼ cup milk**
- **1 cup torn sliced white bread, densely packed**
- **1 small onion, roughly chopped**
- **6 cloves fresh garlic, roughly chopped**
- **Leaves from 2 stalks of fresh oregano or**
  2 tablespoons dried oregano
- **10 fresh mint leaves**
- **1 tablespoon salt**
- **Freshly ground black pepper**
- **1 pound lean ground beef**
- **Rice (for serving)**
- **Plain yogurt (for serving)**
- **Fresh lemon juice (for serving)**
- **Garnish (recipe follows)**

Serves 4

▲ ■ ● ▲ ■ ● ▲ ■ ● ▲

1. Preheat oven to 350°F.

2. In the food processor, combine and process all the ingredients except the ground beef and garnish. Add the beef and process until combined, stopping if necessary to scrape the ingredients away from the sides of the processor and into the center. (A rubber spatula works best for this.)

3. Unplug the food processor, remove blade, and shape the mixture into meatballs. To shape into perfect balls, roll each meatball between both palms. They can be big or small—it doesn't matter, as long as they're all the same size so they will cook evenly.

4. Place meatballs on a sheet pan lined with parchment paper or aluminum foil, and bake until browned and cooked through. Large meatballs take longer to cook than small meatballs.

5. Serve over rice and top with a dollop of plain room-temperature yogurt. Sprinkle with Garnish and a bit of fresh lemon juice.

Garnish

Ingredients

- 1 cucumber, peeled, seeded, diced
- 1 tomato, diced
- ⅛ red onion, diced
- Juice of ½ lemon
- Salt
- Freshly ground black pepper

1. In a small bowl, combine all the garnish ingredients, and toss with the lemon juice. Season with salt and pepper.

Seeding cucumbers

To seed the cucumber, first peel it with a vegetable peeler. Then ask an adult to slice off the ends and cut it in half lengthwise. With a spoon, scoop out the seeds so the cucumber forms the shape of a canoe.

Why is this a good garnish?

The garnish is good because it's colorful and attractive. Food tastes better when it looks good. Think of it like this—would you rather drive a brown station wagon or a cherry red convertible?

Falaf-A-Balls

Gear

- Colander
- Measuring cups
- Measuring spoons
- Food processor
- Rubber spatula
- Sheet pan
- Parchment paper or aluminum foil
- Paper towels
- Oven mitts
- Pastry brush
- 2 medium bowls
- Spoon

Ingredients

- 2 13- to 15-ounce cans garbanzo beans
  (chick peas), drained and rinsed in a colander
- 4 cloves fresh garlic, roughly chopped
- 2 eggs
- 1½ to 2 cups all-purpose flour
- 2 tablespoons breadcrumbs
- 2 stalks celery, roughly chopped
- 2 scallions, roughly chopped
- ¾ teaspoon ground cumin
- ¾ teaspoon ground coriander
- ½ cup roughly chopped fresh Italian (flat-leaf)
  parsley
- ¼ teaspoon cayenne
- 2 teaspoons salt
- 1 teaspoon freshly ground black pepper
- ½ cup vegetable oil
- 1 package pita bread
- Sauce (recipe follows)
- Garnish (recipe follows)

Serves 6 to 8

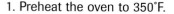

1. Preheat the oven to 350°F.

2. In a food processor, combine all ingredients except oil, pita, Garnish, and Sauce. Purée until smooth, stopping if necessary to scrape the ingredients away from the sides of the processor and into the center. (A rubber spatula works best for this.)

3. Line a sheet pan with parchment paper or aluminum foil. With a paper towel, spread a thin layer of oil over the parchment or foil.

4. Unplug the food processor and remove the blade. With floured hands, form 1-inch balls of batter and place them onto the oiled sheet pan. Cook for 30 minutes, until Falaf-a-Balls are crispy on the outside. If you'd like, about half way through the cooking process, remove the pan from the oven and use a pastry brush to brush the balls with oil. Then continue to bake until browned and crispy.

5. Ask an adult to cut the pitas in half to form two separate pockets.

6. After the Falaf-a-Balls are done cooking, place pitas in oven to warm, about 2 to 3 minutes.

7. To eat, place a few falafel balls in a pita pocket, top with Sauce, and then with Garnish.

What's the Difference Between an Herb and a Spice?

An herb comes from the leaf of a plant. A spice comes from the seed or bark of a plant.

Garnish

Ingredients

2 tomatoes, finely diced

1 cucumber, peeled, seeded, finely chopped

¾ cup finely diced red onion

1. In a medium bowl, combine all ingredients.

Sauce

Ingredients

½ cup tahini

1½ cups plain yogurt

Juice of 2 lemons

¼ cup finely chopped fresh Italian (flat-leaf) parsley, stems removed

4 cloves fresh garlic, minced

2 teaspoons salt

2 teaspoons freshly ground black pepper

¼ teaspoon cayenne

1. In a medium bowl, combine all ingredients.

Mexiballs

Gear

- Measuring cups
- Measuring spoons
- Long-handled tongs (about 10 inches)
- Baking sheet (optional)
- Large saucepan
- Kitchen scissors
- Medium bowl
- 2 sheet pans
- Oven mitts
- Food processor
- Rubber spatula
- Parchment paper or aluminum foil
- 4 serving bowls
- Spoon or spatula

Ingredients for Broth

- 2 Anaheim chile peppers
- 2 tablespoons cooking oil
- 2 scallions, finely chopped
- 1 14.5-ounce can chopped tomatoes, drained
- 1 tablespoon all-purpose flour
- 2 cloves of fresh garlic, finely chopped
- 4 cups (1 quart) chicken stock

Serves 4

1. Roasting chiles on the stovetop is fun and not dangerous as long as the right tool is used: in this case, a pair of long-handled tongs. If you have a gas stove, turn the flame to high, and hold the chile directly over the fire. Cook until the chile blisters and turns black. It will snap, crackle, and pop, just like Rice Krispies cereal. Using tongs, keep turning the chile so that all sides are charred. If the chile turns gray, it has cooked too long. If you only have an electric stove, you can do this under the broiler or outside over the grill. For broiling, place an oven rack 3 to 5 inches from the broiler, then preheat the broiler. Place the chiles on a baking sheet, and place baking sheet on oven rack. Leave oven door open. When one side of chiles are blackened, remove baking sheet, and rotate chiles. Place back under broiler. Repeat until chiles are blackened all over.

2. Remove the chiles from heat, and cool. When cool, place under cold, running water, and gently rub the skins off. Then ask an adult to cut off the stem, and remove all the seeds from inside. Ask an adult to finely chop the chiles, discarding the stems and seeds.*

*Important Note: After this process, you will have the oil from the chiles on your fingers. It is very important that you not touch your eyes or any sensitive area of your body until this oil has been removed. It is normally not enough just to wash your hands. It's best to take a shower or bath.

3. Heat the oil in a large saucepan over moderate heat. Add the scallions, tomatoes, and chopped chiles. Lightly sprinkle the flour all over the vegetables, and cook for about 5 minutes, stirring occasionally.

4. Add the garlic. Cook for 1 minute, then add the chicken stock before the garlic burns.

5. Bring the broth to a boil, reduce heat to medium, and cook for another 5 to 10 minutes.

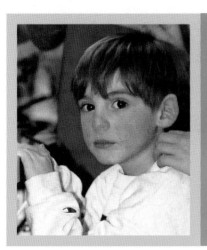

Tortillas

Ingredients
10 corn tortillas
¼ cup cooking oil

1. Preheat oven to 350°F.

2. While the broth is cooking, use a pair of kitchen scissors to cut the tortillas into thin strips. Place in a medium bowl and add oil. Toss well to coat the tortilla strips evenly with oil.

3. Spread on a sheet pan, and place in the oven until crispy, about 15 minutes. Remove from oven, and set aside.

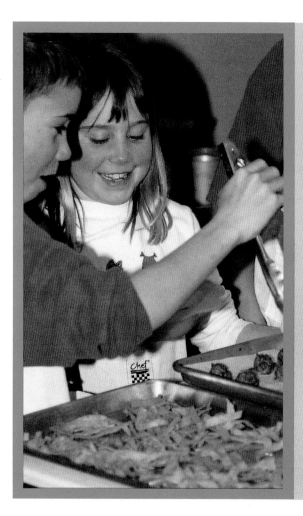

Meatballs

Ingredients

- ¼ cup masa harina or flour (see below)
- 3 fresh garlic cloves, rough-chopped
- 1 tablespoon salt
- 1 teaspoon freshly ground black pepper
- 1 egg
- ½ pound ground beef
- Salt to taste
- ¼ bunch cilantro, chopped (for serving)

1. Preheat oven to 450°F.

2. In the food processor, combine all the meatball ingredients except the ground beef and cilantro. Then add the beef, and process until combined, stopping if necessary to scrape the ingredients away from the sides of the processor and into the center. (A rubber spatula works best for this.) Unplug the food processor, remove the blade, and form the mixture into small meatballs. To shape into perfect balls, roll each meatball between both palms. The actual size does not matter, as long as they're the same, so they'll cook evenly.

3. Place the meatballs on a sheet pan lined with parchment paper or aluminum foil, and bake until browned, about 10 minutes.

4. Remove from oven, and add the meatballs to the stock to finish cooking, about 10 minutes.

5. Place tortilla strips in the bottom of four serving bowls. Add meatballs and soup.

6. Salt to taste. Garnish at the table with fresh cilantro.

Masa harina is a Mexican "flour" made of ground corn and lime. It can be found in the Mexican food section of most markets. If you can't find it, no problem—just substitute flour.

Shish for your Kabob

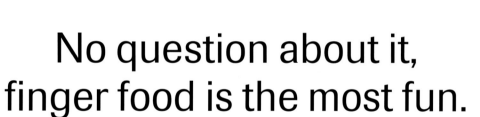

No question about it,
finger food is the most fun.

French Toast Kebobs with Fresh Fruit

Gear

Medium bowl
Whisk
Paper towel
Sheet pan
12 wooden skewers
Oven Mitts

Ingredients

4 eggs
1½ cups milk
1 tablespoon vanilla
Zest of 1 orange, lemon, or lime
1 loaf unsliced quality white bread (a little stale is okay)
1 or 2 tablespoons butter or oil
½ pint strawberries, rinsed and drained, stemmed, halved
½ pint blueberries, rinsed and drained
Maple syrup (for serving)
Powdered sugar (for serving)

Serves 4 to 6

Add Zest for Zing!

Zest, which is the colored, outer skin of citrus fruits like lemons, limes, and oranges, adds zing to your dishes. When cooking with zest, it's important to cook with only the colored part of the skin and not the bitter white pith underneath. A special tool called a "zester" is the best way to get just the amount of skin that you need. If you don't have a zester, you can use a vegetable peeler, but take care to trim away the white pith!

1. Preheat oven to 350°F.

2. In a medium bowl, with a whisk, combine eggs and milk. Add vanilla and zest. Set the mixture aside.

3. Ask an adult to use a bread knife to cut the bread into 2-inch cubes.

4. Use a paper towel to spread butter or oil on a sheet pan.

5. Place one handful of cubed bread in milk-egg mixture. Working fairly quickly, skewer 1 cube of bread, followed by ½ a strawberry, followed by 1 bread cube, then 1 blueberry, 1 bread cube, ½ a strawberry, 1 bread cube, 1 blueberry, 1 bread cube, etc., until only 1 inch remains at the pointed end of the skewer.

6. Place full skewer on the buttered pan and repeat step 5 until all bread cubes are gone.

7. Make sure that the fruit does not touch the pan—only the bread should touch the tray. The fruit will cook from the heat of the oven, but if it is allowed to touch the tray, the juices from the fruit will seep out and make the bread soggy.

8. Place in the oven and bake until the bread is golden brown, about 20 to 30 minutes.

9. To serve, drizzle with maple syrup and sprinkle with powdered sugar.

Fajita Bobs

Gear

Wooden or metal skewers
Measuring cups
Measuring spoons
Sheet pan (if broiling)
Parchment paper (if broiling)
Plastic or glass container with lid
Juicer
Spoon

Ingredients

1 pound flank steak
Marinade (recipe follows)
1 yellow bell pepper, cut into 1-inch squares
1 red bell pepper, cut into 1-inch squares
1 red onion, cut into 1-inch squares
8 tortillas
Guacamole, or peeled sliced avocado (for serving)
Sour cream (for serving)
Salsa (for serving)

Before You Grill . . .
It is important to soak
wooden skewers in water.
Otherwise, they may burn on
the grill or under the broiler.

Serves 4

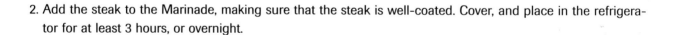

1. Have an adult slice flank steak across the grain into thin strips, ¼- to ⅛-inch thick.

2. Add the steak to the Marinade, making sure that the steak is well-coated. Cover, and place in the refrigerator for at least 3 hours, or overnight.

3. When ready to cook, preheat the grill or broiler to high heat.

4. Skewer the steak strips, alternating with pepper and onion squares. Cook on the grill or under the broiler until the meat is nicely browned, 3 to 5 minutes per side. Remember to turn the meat after one side has browned, so that the opposite side cooks evenly. If using the broiler, cover a sheet pan with parchment paper, place the Fajita Bobs on top, and follow the instructions above.

5. Quickly warm the tortillas to soften them, either on the grill after it has been shut off or in the oven with the broiler shut off.

6. Place a skewer over a warmed tortilla. Spoon some guacamole, sour cream, and/or salsa over it. Roll tortilla around kabob, grip firmly, and remove skewer. Eat!

Marinade

Ingredients

- Juice of 2 oranges
- Juice of 1 lime
- Juice of 1 lemon
- 6 cloves fresh garlic, smashed
- $\frac{1}{3}$ cup white or brown sugar
- 1 jalapeño chile, quartered
- $\frac{1}{4}$ cup fresh oregano leaves, gently packed

1. In a large plastic or glass container, combine all the ingredients. Set aside.

Wake up and Hear the Juice!
A juicer turns your favorite citrus into juice. Its sound in the morning is as welcoming as the smell of bacon.

Chicken Teriyaki Kabobs

Gear

Wooden or metal skewers

Oven mitts

Measuring cups

Measuring spoons

Sheet pan

Parchment paper or aluminum foil

Blender

Rubber spatula

Plastic or glass container with lid

Ingredients

1 pound boneless chicken, cut in 2-inch chunks

Marinade (recipe follows)

1 14-ounce can chunk pineapple

1 red or yellow bell pepper, seeded, cut in chunks

1 yellow onion, peeled, cut in chunks

Rice (for serving)

Serves 4

1. Place the chicken in a plastic or glass container with the Marinade, making sure the chicken is well-coated. Cover, and place in the refrigerator for at least 4 hours, or overnight.

2. Preheat oven to 400°F.

3. Skewer the ingredients, alternating between the chicken, pineapple, bell pepper, and onion. Grill or roast in the oven on parchment paper or foil-lined sheet pan until chicken is browned and cooked through, about 15 minutes.

4. Serve with rice.

Marinade

Ingredients

- 5 scallions, roughly chopped, both white and green parts
- 1 tablespoon peeled, roughly chopped ginger
- 2 garlic cloves, peeled, rough-chopped
- $\frac{1}{2}$ cup soy sauce
- $\frac{1}{4}$ cup brown sugar
- $\frac{1}{4}$ cup sugar

1. Combine all the ingredients in a blender. Set aside.

Is Dinner Ready Yet?

To test whether chicken is ready to eat,
slice into one piece.
The flesh inside should be white, not pink.

Thai-Bobs

Gear

Measuring cups
Measuring spoons
Food processor
Rubber spatula
Wooden or metal skewers
Sheet pan
Parchment paper or aluminum foil
Oven mitts
Juicer
Spoon
Medium saucepan

Ingredients

1 stalk lemongrass, the top ⅔ (the thin part)
   discarded
1 pound ground pork
¼ cup dry bread crumbs
½ cup all-purpose flour
1 egg
¼ cup sugar
1 tablespoon Thai fish sauce
¼ cup roughly chopped onion
3 cloves garlic, roughly chopped
1½ teaspoons cornstarch
8 fresh mint leaves
¼ cup rough-chopped fresh cilantro
1 teaspoon salt
½ teaspoon freshly ground black pepper
1 head Boston lettuce, leaves cut in half
Dipping Sauce (recipe follows)

Serves 4

1. Preheat the oven to 350°F.

2. Ask an adult to chop off the bottom ½-inch of the lemongrass stalk and discard it. Remove the outer layer of the remaining lemongrass stalk, and discard it. Ask an adult to finely chop the remaining lemongrass, and place in food processor.

3. Combine all remaining ingredients, except lettuce and Dipping Sauce, in food processor, stopping if necessary to scrape the ingredients away from the sides of the processor and into the center. (A rubber spatula works best for this.)

4. Unplug the food processor, remove blade, and shape into meatballs. They can be big or small—it doesn't matter, as long as they're all the same size. This way, they will all cook evenly. To shape into perfect balls, roll each meatball between both your palms. Run a skewer through 4 meatballs, and repeat until all are skewered.

5. Place meatballs on a sheet pan lined with parchment paper or aluminum foil, and bake until browned and cooked through. Large meatballs take longer to cook than small meatballs. To test for doneness, use a fork to cut into one meatball. There should be no red color left in the meat.

6. To serve, wrap the individual meatballs in lettuce leaves, and dunk them in the Dipping Sauce.

Dipping Sauce

Ingredients

Juice of 2 fresh limes

2 tablespoons Thai fish sauce

¼ jalapeño chile, not diced

2 tablespoons rice vinegar

½ cup sugar, or more to taste

⅓ cup hot water

¼ cup chopped fresh cilantro

1. Combine all ingredients in a medium saucepan. Bring to a boil, then reduce heat to medium and cook for five minutes or until the sugar is dissolved.

2. Serve at room temperature in small bowls.

Fresh Fruit Animals

Gear

Toothpicks and/or wooden skewers

Ingredients

Fresh fruit

● ▲ ■ ● ▲ ■ ● ▲ ■ ●

1. Use your imagination to create four of your favorite animals or see the examples to the right for animals we've created. You can use any fruit you have around the house—just remember to wash it before using it in your creations. Serve for dessert.

Ole Blue Eyes

1 lemon
2½ strawberries
2 blueberries
2 red grapes
½ green grape
1 apricot

Berry Far from Home

4 raspberries
2 blueberries
1 strawberry
1 lemon or apple wedge

72

Fuzzy Navel
1 kiwi
4 green grapes
1 red grape, sliced in half
1 blackberry
2 blueberries

Bottom Feeder
$\frac{1}{2}$ pineapple
2 kiwi halves
4 oranges

Grazing

It's downright un-American
not to eat snacks!

Tuna Tostadas

Gear

Measuring spoons
Measuring cups
Medium bowl
Baking sheet
Oven mitts
Fork

Ingredients

4 corn tortillas
Tuna Salad (recipe follows)
1 cup grated cheddar cheese

Serves 4

● ▲ ■ ● ▲ ■ ● ▲ ■ ● ▲ ■ ● ▲ ■ ● ▲ ■ ● ▲

1. Preheat the oven to 375°F.

2. Place the tortillas on a baking sheet, and place in the oven until slightly crispy.

3. Remove the tortillas from the oven, and let cool. Spread the Tuna Salad equally onto all four tortillas. Sprinkle equally with cheese.

5. Place back in the oven, and cook just until the cheese is bubbly.

Tuna Salad

Ingredients

1 12-ounce can tuna drained
2 stalks celery, finely chopped
1 cup shredded iceberg lettuce
$\frac{1}{2}$ cup mayonnaise
$1\frac{1}{2}$ tablespoons sweet pickle relish

1. In a medium bowl, combine all ingredients with a fork. Keep in refrigerator until you're ready to use.

Lucky Duck

Gear

- Measuring spoons
- Paper towels
- Large oven-safe saucepan with tight-fitting lid or Dutch oven
- Oven mitts
- Tongs
- Slotted spoon
- 2 forks
- Plastic container with lid
- Frying pan
- Microwave-safe plate (optional)

Ingredients

- 1 whole duck
- Water or chicken stock
- Scallions, chopped in 1-inch lengths
- 2 to 3 tablespoons cooking oil
- Hoisin sauce (available in your market's Asian food section)
- Mandarin pancakes for Peking duck (Ask your favorite Chinese restaurant to let you take some home. If they won't, use a thin variety of flour tortillas and find a new favorite Chinese restaurant.)

Serves 8

1. Preheat oven to 275°F.

2. Remove the neck and giblets (the gizzard, liver, heart, and neck) from inside the duck. Rinse with cold water. Pat very dry with paper towels.

3. Place the duck in a large saucepan. Add water, stock, or a combination of both until a third of the duck is covered. Cover the saucepan with a tight-fitting lid. Place in oven for at least 6 hours or overnight. Wash your hands well with soap and water after handling the duck.

4. Remove the saucepan from the oven. Use tongs and a slotted spoon to remove the duck from the saucepan, and let cool enough to handle.

5. Using 2 forks (or your fingers!), shred meat from duck, and store in refrigerator in a plastic container with a lid. Discard fat, skin, bones, and carcass. Shredding is fun and easy—just peel small, "stringy" pieces of meat away from the whole duck.

6. When you're ready to serve the duck, heat enough cooking oil to cover the bottom of a large frying pan,* and refry shredded duck until it's hot and crispy. Don't move the duck around too much in the frying pan. Let it become brown and crispy, stirring it only once or twice while it cooks, for about 5 minutes.

7. Serve with bowls of scallions, hoisin sauce, and pancakes. Place some duck, scallions, and hoisin in your pancake, and roll like a burrito!

*If you're not yet comfortable at the stovetop, have an adult fry the duck in advance, and store it in the refrigerator. To serve, place a pancake on a micro-wave-safe plate. Place some duck, scallions, and hoisin in your pancake, and roll like a burrito! Heat in the microwave for 1 or 2 minutes.

A Simple Snack

Surprisingly, this may be the easiest of all the snacks in this chapter. The idea is that on Friday night, you and an adult throw the duck in the oven. On Saturday morning, in just ten minutes time, you've got a snack to enjoy anytime you want, even after school.

Presto Pesto

Gear

- **Measuring cups**
- **Measuring spoons**
- **Baking sheet**
- **Oven mitts**
- **Food processor**
- **Medium saucepan**

Ingredients

- **¼ cup nuts (preferably pine nuts, but walnuts, almonds, and hazelnuts work too!)**
- **¼ pound Parmesan cheese, preferably Parmigiano-Reggiano**
- **2 cups fresh basil leaves, densely packed into measuring cup**
- **1 clove fresh garlic, quartered**
- **¼ to ½ cup olive oil**
- **1 pinch salt**
- **1 jar of your favorite "red" spaghetti sauce**
- **Your favorite cooked pasta**

Serves lots!

● ▲ ■ ● ▲ ■ ● ▲ ■ ● ▲ ■ ● ▲ ■ ● ▲ ■ ● ▲

1. Preheat the oven to 350°F.

2. Spread the nuts onto a dry baking sheet, and place in the oven for just a few minutes until they turn a golden color, taking care not to let them burn. You just want them to toast, so watch them carefully.

3. Use the grater attachment on your food processor to grate enough Parmesan to give you ¼ cup. Unplug the food processor and switch it to the chopping attachment, plug it back in, and add the roasted nuts, basil, garlic, ¼ cup of the oil, and salt to the grated Parmesan.

4. Pulse until a paste forms. You may have to add more oil to get this consistency. Add a little at a time, if necessary. Unplug the food processor.

5. In a medium saucepan, combine the red sauce with the pesto. Simmer over moderate heat until hot about 5 minutes, stirring occasionally.

6. Serve over your favorite pasta.

Drumettes

Gear

Measuring spoons
Measuring cups
Small saucepan
2 large bowls
Sheet pan
Parchment paper or aluminum foil
Oven mitts
2 small bowls
Spoon
Medium bowl
Juicer
Food processor
Rubber spatula

Ingredients

24 chicken drumettes
½ cup (1 stick) butter
1½ tablespoons brown sugar
About 3 tablespoons Tabasco, Durkee's, or other similar hot sauce
Dry Rub (recipe follows)
2 tablespoons tomato sauce
Blue Cheese Dressing (recipe follows)
Celery sticks (for serving)
Carrot sticks (for serving)

Serves 4

1. Set the drumettes out to reach room temperature, no longer than 15 minutes.

2. In a small saucepan, over low heat, melt half of the butter with the brown sugar and half the Tabasco until the sugar dissolves.

4. Add the chicken drumettes to the large bowl with half of the Dry Rub. Using your hands, toss the chicken in the seasonings. Use your thumbs and fingers to really rub it in.

5. Add the butter-and-Tabasco mixture to the wings, and toss the wings in the manner above, this time rubbing the mixture into the wings. Cover and marinate in the refrigerator for about 30 minutes, or marinate them during the first half of a football game and bake them during halftime.

6. Preheat the oven to 375°F. Spread the wings on a sheet pan covered with parchment paper or aluminum foil, and bake until golden brown and crispy, about 20 minutes. Remove and turn once after 10 minutes.

7. Meanwhile, in a small bowl melt the remaining butter with the remaining Tabasco and tomato sauce. Add remaining Dry Rub. Stir until well combined.

8. Place the wings in a large bowl. Pour sauce over wings. Toss to coat evenly. Serve with Blue Cheese Dressing, celery, and carrot sticks.

Dry Rub

Ingredients

- 4 teaspoons salt
- 4 teaspoons paprika
- 2 teaspoons cayenne
- 2 teaspoons onion powder
- 2 teaspoons garlic powder
- 1½ teaspoons white pepper

1. In a medium bowl combine all the ingredients. Reserve half the dry rub mixture in a small bowl, and set aside for the sauce. You'll use the remaining mixture for the chicken.

Blue Cheese Dressing

Ingredients

- ½ cup sour cream
- ½ cup mayonnaise
- ½ cup crumbled blue cheese
- Juice of ¼ lemon
- 1 tablespoon cider vinegar
- 2 scallions, roughly chopped
- 1 stalk celery, roughly chopped
- 1 teaspoon salt
- 1 teaspoon freshly-ground black pepper
- ⅛ teaspoon cayenne
- 1 teaspoon Worcestershire sauce

1. Combine all ingredients in a food processor, and purée until dressing is the texture you prefer. You may have to stop occasionally to use a rubber spatula to scrape all the ingredients from the side of the processor back into the center.

2. Unplug the food processor and use a rubber spatula to transfer the dressing to a serving bowl. Serve with the Drumettes.

Chocolate Nachos

Gear

- **Measuring cups**
- **Measuring spoons**
- **Medium bowl**
- **Kitchen scissors**
- **Baking sheet**
- **Small microwave-safe glass bowl**
- **Pastry brush**
- **Oven mitts**
- **Spatula**

Ingredients

- **¼ cup sugar**
- **2 teaspoons ground cinnamon**
- **2 large flour tortillas**
- **2 tablespoons butter (¼ stick)**
- **Chocolate syrup, room temperature**
- **Whipped cream**

Serves 2

1. Preheat oven to 400°F.

2. In a medium bowl, combine the sugar and cinnamon.

3. Use a pair of kitchen scissors to cut the tortillas into thick strips or triangles. Place the tortilla strips on a baking sheet.

4. Place the butter in a microwave-safe glass bowl, and microwave about 20 seconds on high, until melted.

5. Use a pastry brush to brush the tortilla strips entirely with melted butter. You might not use all of the butter—just enough to thoroughly coat each strip.

6. Sprinkle the strips with cinnamon-sugar (you might not use all of it).

7. Bake for 5 to 10 minutes, or until the strips are crispy. Remove the baking sheet from the oven.

8. Using a spatula, move the strips from the baking sheet to serving plates.

9. Pour chocolate syrup over tortilla strips. Top with whipped cream.

Microwave Safety

Microwaves can pass through glass and plastic, but not through metal, which can be extremely dangerous if placed in the microwave. *Always* use a microwave-safe bowl or dish in the microwave.

Peanut Butter Universe

Gear

- Measuring cups
- Measuring spoons
- Paper towel
- Baking sheet
- Large bowl
- Spoon
- Medium saucepan

Ingredients

- 1 tablespoon butter
- 2½ cups toasted rice cereal
- 2¼ cups rolled oats
- ¾ cup chopped dry roasted, salted peanuts
- ¼ cup semisweet chocolate chips
- ¼ cup flaked coconut
- ½ cup creamy peanut butter
- ¾ cup firmly packed brown sugar
- ¾ cup light corn syrup
- 1 teaspoon vanilla extract

Makes 9 snacks

● ▲ ■ ● ▲ ■ ● ▲ ■ ● ▲ ■ ● ▲ ■ ● ▲ ■ ● ▲

1. Place butter on a wadded-up paper towel, and coat the baking sheet.

2. In a large bowl, combine the cereal, oats, peanuts, chocolate chips, and coconut.

3. Combine peanut butter, brown sugar, corn syrup, and vanilla in a medium saucepan over low heat. Stir occasionally, until the mixture just begins to boil.

4. Pour over the cereal mixture. Stir with a spoon to mix well. When cool enough, finish mixing with your hands.

5. Spoon onto buttered baking sheet, and, using the tips of your fingers, press the mixture together until it is flat, level, and pressed to the sides.

6. Allow to cool to room temperature, then ask an adult to cut into bars. Wrap individually in plastic wrap, and take to school, or store at home in an airtight container.

Marshmallow Sushi

Gear
Hands and fingers!

Ingredients
4 dried fruit roll-ups

16 large marshmallows

Makes 4 Sushi Rolls

● ▲ ■ ● ▲ ■ ● ▲ ▲ ■ ● ▲ ▲ ● ▲ ■ ● ▲ ▲ ■ ● ▲

1. Ask an adult to cut fruit roll-ups into flat sheets 4 to 6 inches wide and 6 to 8 inches tall, which is about the size of a sheet of nori (toasted seaweed traditionally used to make sushi).

2. Place as many marshmallows as possible along the bottom edge of the fruit roll-up. Roll the marshmallows tightly inside the fruit roll-up.

3. Ask an adult to cut into slices approximately ½-inch to ¾-inch thick, which is about the thickness of rolled sushi.

Hedgehog Truffles

Gear
Double boiler
Medium bowl
Teaspoon

Ingredients
½ cup semi-sweet chocolate chips
1 tablespoon butter
1 teaspoon vegetable shortening
2 tablespoons heavy cream or milk
1 teaspoon hazelnut oil (optional)
8 to 9 teaspoons powdered sugar
2 tablespoons finely chopped hazelnuts
3 tablespoons chocolate shot
1 tablespoon butterscotch bits

Makes about 20 hedgehogs

1. Place chocolate chips and butter in the bowl of a double boiler, and heat until the water starts to boil. If you don't have a double boiler, make your own by following the directions on page 43.

2. Reduce heat to low, and melt the chocolate, butter, and shortening. While the chocolate is melting, add the cream or milk, powdered sugar, and hazelnuts and stir it into the mixture. Take care not to allow any water to get into the bowl of chocolate, as this will change the chocolate to a solid again.

3. Set aside to let the mixture cool, then place in the refrigerator for one hour.

4. Place the chocolate shot in a medium bowl.

5. Use a teaspoon to scoop a small ball of chocolate. Roll it in your hands to form an oval shape.

6. Roll the chocolate balls in the shot to cover, tapping lightly to knock off the excess. Gently press in a butterscotch chip for the nose.

7. Repeat steps 5 and 6 to make the rest of the hedgehogs. Allow them to rest in the refrigerator until you're ready to eat them.

Show Me the Money

Cheddar Pennies

Gear
- Measuring cups
- Measuring spoons
- Standing mixer
- Waxed paper or parchment paper
- Cookie sheets
- Baking rack
- Oven mitts

Ingredients
- 1 pound sharp cheddar cheese, grated
- 6 tablespoons ($^3/_4$ stick) unsalted butter or margarine
- 2 cups all-purpose flour
- 1 teaspoon salt
- $^1/_2$ teaspoon red pepper
- Paprika

Makes about $1.00

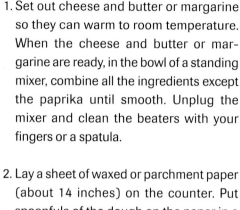

1. Set out cheese and butter or margarine so they can warm to room temperature. When the cheese and butter or margarine are ready, in the bowl of a standing mixer, combine all the ingredients except the paprika until smooth. Unplug the mixer and clean the beaters with your fingers or a spatula.

2. Lay a sheet of waxed or parchment paper (about 14 inches) on the counter. Put spoonfuls of the dough on the paper in a line to form a 1-inch thick "snake" of dough. Using your hands, roll the dough back and forth to get it smooth and even. Roll the snake in the waxed paper and twist the ends to close. Place the snake in the refrigerator. Repeat until all the dough is formed into snakes and placed in the refrigerator. Let the dough chill for 1 hour.

3. Preheat the oven to 350°F.

4. Remove the cheese snakes from the refrigerator and unwrap them. Ask an adult to slice into cheddar pennies about $^1/_8$- to $^1/_4$-inch thick. Don't slice them too thick or you'll be shortchanged!

5. Place them on a cookie sheet lined with parchment paper. Sprinkle lightly with paprika. Bake about 10 to 12 minutes, until golden brown. Remove from the pan and cool on a baking rack or on the parchment paper.

Ginger Nickels

Gear

Measuring cups
Measuring spoons
Standing mixer
Mixing bowl
Large bowl
Sifter
Waxed paper or parchment paper
Spoon
Cookie sheets
Oven mitts
Baking rack

Ingredients

1 cup (2 sticks) unsalted butter
1 cup sugar
1 cup dark molasses
1 egg
½ teaspoon vanilla extract
4 cups all-purpose flour
1 teaspoon baking soda
1 teaspoon salt
2 teaspoons ground cinnamon
1 teaspoon ground ginger
½ teaspoon ground mace
¼ teaspoon ground cloves

Makes about $1.50

● ▲ ■ ● ▲ ■ ● ▲

These cookies taste best dunked in a cold glass of milk.

1. In the bowl of a standing mixer, cream the butter and sugar until smooth. Add the molasses, egg, and vanilla, and continue mixing until smooth.

2. In a separate large bowl, sift together the flour, baking soda, salt, cinnamon, ginger, mace, and cloves. Add this to the creamed mixture in small amounts, each time combining until smooth. Unplug the mixer and clean the beaters with your fingers or a rubber spatula.

3. Lay a sheet of waxed or parchment paper (about 14 inches) on the counter. Put spoonfuls of the ginger dough on the paper in a line to form a 1-inch thick "snake" of dough. Using your hands, roll the dough back and forth to get it smooth and even. Roll the snake in the waxed paper and twist the ends to close. Place the snake in the freezer. Repeat until all the dough is formed into snakes and placed in the freezer. Let the dough chill for 30 minutes.

4. Preheat oven to 350°F.

5. Take a snake out, unwrap it, and ask an adult to slice it thinly. Place the slices on cookie sheets and bake for 7 to 9 minutes.

6. If you would like to save the cookies for a later time, the snakes should be put in a zipper-lock bag and kept in the freezer until ready to slice and bake.

Glossary

Batter: A spoonable mixture of wet and dry ingredients.

Beat: To stir vigorously with a fork, hand-held whisk, or electric beaters.

Blanch and shock: If you like bright colors, you'll love this technique. Usually used for vegetables, it requires briefly submerging them in boiling water, then removing them and immediately submerging them in ice water. The color of the vegetable becomes brighter after it is shocked, and the brief cooking gives the vegetable a nice crispness.

Broth: For our puposes, broth is the same as stock, which can either be purchased at the grocery store in the soup aisle, or prepared at home by simmering meaty bones and aromatic vegetables.

Brown: In the case of cooking, brown is the opposite of gray. When meats are cooked properly, their surfaces are crispy and brown, not gray and dull as they are when they're undercooked.

Chop: Most of the recipes in this book call for "rough-chopping," which requires that ingredients be cut into small to medium-size pieces. "Fine chops" require that food be cut into very small pieces.

Cooking oil: Cooking oil is meant to be distinguished from finishing oils like extra virgin olive oil or infused oils, which are expensive and high in flavor. The best cooking oil is grapeseed oil, but vegetable or canola oils also work well.

Core: To remove the center of a fruit, specifically its seeds or pit.

Cream: To whip butter and sugar until light and fluffy.

Dice: To chop into square pieces. Can be a small, medium, or large dice.

Dissolve: When one ingredient disappears inside another. For example, sugar dissolves in water.

Dough: Dough is similar to batter, but thicker in consistency.

Drizzle: To pour only a limited amount in a small, thin stream.

Flour, all-purpose: *All-purpose* is printed right on the bag of flour, to distinguish it from other types of flour, such as *whole wheat, bleached, sifted,* etc. This is the most common kind of flour.

Fold: A slow, gentle stirring motion with a rubber spatula that entails cutting through a bowl of ingredients to the bowl's bottom and combining ingredients by lifting from underneath.

Garlic clove: Don't confuse a clove with a bulb of garlic; otherwise, you'll quickly alienate your friends and family with your breath. A bulb is made up of lots of cloves. Most recipes call for a specified number of cloves.

Garnish: Used to decorate food and add to or complement its flavor.

Glaze: A mixture that makes food shiny.

Grate: To shred, as with cheese.

Grease: To use butter or oil to keep other ingredients from sticking to a baking dish or frying pan.

Knead: To "work" dough with your hands.

Marinate: Soaking meats or vegetables in a flavorful combination of ingredients prior to cooking. The flavors of the ingredients, or *marinade*, are absorbed by the meat or vegetable.

Mince: To finely dice.

Preheat oven: To turn your oven to a specific temperature 10 to 15 minutes prior to using it to bake or roast, and 5 minutes prior to using it to broil.

Pulp: The flesh or "meat" inside a fruit or vegetable. When its pulp is removed, a fruit or vegetable is made hollow, like a basket into which you can put your favorite things—in this case, your favorite ingredients.

Pulse: Some appliances have pulse switches in addition to an on/off switch. Of course, on/off allows you to turn things on and off. The pulse switch gives you a little more control. Try it, and find out whether or not you're a control freak.

Purée: To make into a smooth paste.

Reduce: To decrease the amount of liquid in a saucepan in order to concentrate flavors. For example, if you start with 2 cups of liquid, and a recipe says to reduce by half, you will boil the 2 cups of liquid until approximately 1 cup remains.

Room temperature: The same temperature as your house, about 68 to 70°F.

Sift: To combine using a sifter, which is a mesh-bottomed kitchen tool.

Skewer: 1. *(verb)* The process of arranging food onto a skewer. **2.** *(noun)* A thin wooden or metal rod onto which cubes or chunks of food are arranged for cooking.

Smash: A highly technical term that usually refers to crushing a garlic clove by holding the flat side of a table knife on top of the garlic in one hand and using the other hand to smash the knife into the garlic.

Sugar, confectioner's: Refers to powdered sugar.

Toast: To make food brown and crisp.

Toss: To mix quickly and lightly with two utensils or hands.

Whip: To stir vigorously with a whisk, electric beater, or electric mixer with a whip attachment.

Whisk: To mix using a whisk.

Zest: To remove the skin of a citrus fruit by grating finely. The idea is to remove the colored skin but not the white pith underneath, which is bitter.

Conversion Tables

Generic Formulas for Metric Conversion

Ounces to grams	multiply ounces by 28.35
Pounds to grams	multiply pounds by 453.5
Cups to liters	multiply cups by .24
Fahrenheit to Centigrade	subtract 32 from Fahrenheit, multiply by five and divide by 9

Metric Equivalents for Volume

U.S.	Imperial	Metric
1/8 tsp.	–	.6 mL
1/2 tsp.	–	2.5 mL
3/4 tsp.	–	4.0 mL
1 tsp.	–	5.0 mL
1 1/2 tsp.	–	7.0 mL
2 tsp.	–	10.0 mL
3 tsp.	–	15.0 mL
4 tsp.	–	20.0 mL
1 Tbsp.	–	15.0 mL
1 1/2 Tbsp.	–	22.0 mL
2 Tbsp. (1/8 cup)	1 fl. oz	30.0 mL
2 1/2 Tbsp.	–	37.0 mL
3 Tbsp.	–	44.0 mL
1/3 cup	–	57.0 mL
4 Tbsp. (1/4 cup)	2 fl. oz	59.0 mL
5 Tbsp.	–	74.0 mL
6 Tbsp.	–	89.0 mL
8 Tbsp. (1/2 cup)	4 fl. oz	120.0 mL
3/4 cup	6 fl. oz	178.0 mL
1 cup	8 fl. oz	237.0 mL (.24 liters)
1 1/2 cups	–	354.0 mL
1 3/4 cups	–	414.0 mL
2 cups (1 pint)	16 fl. oz	473.0 mL
4 cups (1 quart)	32 fl. oz	(.95 liters)
5 cups	–	1185.0 mL (1.183 liters)
16 cups (1 gallon)	128 fl. oz	(3.8 liters)

Oven Temperatures

Degrees Fahrenheit	Degrees Centigrade	British Gas Marks
200°	93.0°	–
250°	120.0°	–
275°	140.0°	1
300°	150.0°	2
325°	165.0°	3
350°	175.0°	4
375°	190.0°	5
400°	200.0°	6
450°	230.0°	8

Metric Equivalents for Weight

U.S.	Metric
1 oz	28 g
2 oz	58 g
3 oz	85 g
4 oz (1/4 lb.)	113 g
5 oz	142 g
6 oz	170 g
7 oz	199 g
8 oz (1/2 lb.)	227 g
10 oz	284 g
12 oz (3/4 lb.)	340 g
14 oz	397 g
16 oz (1 lb.)	454 g

Metric Equivalents for Butter

U.S	Metric
2 tsp.	10.0 g
1 Tbsp.	15.0 g
1 1/2 Tbsp.	22.5 g
2 Tbsp. (1 oz)	55.0 g
3 Tbsp.	70.0 g
1/4 lb. (1 stick)	110.0 g
1/2 lb. (2 sticks)	220.0 g

Metric Equivalents for Length (use also for pan sizes)

U.S.	Metric
1/4 inch	.65 cm
1/2 inch	1.25 cm
1 inch	2.50 cm
2 inches	5.00 cm
3 inches	6.00 cm
4 inches	8.00 cm
5 inches	11.00 cm
6 inches	15.00 cm
7 inches	18.00 cm
8 inches	20.00 cm
9 inches	23.00 cm
12 inches	30.50 cm
15 inches	38.00 cm

Index

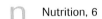

About the Author

Rob Seideman is the president and founder of the nationally recognized Cooking School of Aspen in Aspen, Colorado. Rob teaches all of the very popular children's classes, which have received national attention for years—in March 2000, *Gourmet* magazine wrote that it was "one of the most talked-about kids programs in the country." Rob's approach to teaching children to cook is nontraditional, with a focus on challenging children to learn to make dishes that will fill them with pride and a desire to continue to cook. Rob lives in Aspen with his family.